MISSING QUINN

Manufactured in the United States of America.

Cover work by Sherri Rowland.

First Edition

ISBN: 978-0-9968392-0-4

MISSING QUINN

Surviving Loss
and
Understanding Parents in Grief

Susanne E. Levi

Dedication

To Quinn and Will, my amazing sons. The days you were born were the best days of my life.

Gratitudes

Will, you inspire me to live, and I am so proud of you and the young man you have become despite our families tragedy. Quinn, I will see you again and long for the hugs I have been missing. My husband, Bill, we are in this together, no one understands like you do, and I love you. And to my friends, Taunya, Claudia and Nancy thanks for never giving up on me and always listening.

CONTENTS

INTRODUCTION

PART ONE OUR STORY

PART TWO - ADVICE

Introduction

I wrote this book over a period of five years. As you read you will hear my raw sadness and anger from the day this tragedy destroyed my family. I never wanted to know how many days, weeks or years had passed since the day my son and father were taken from me. Honestly, for a very long time I didn't understand how or why I was still here. With the help of a lot of caring friends, family and therapy I realized why I was needed to still be here. I had to make the decision to live. I hope you feel my sadness and anger, but most of all, I hope you see how our lives can change in a second. I hope you have a better understanding of what you can do to help a grieving family. Take the time to enjoy your children, help others and live life without wishing what you would have done.

About Us

I grew up in Pennsylvania with my sister, Donna, and my mom and dad. We lived in a nice house where the neighbors all knew each other, and kids could play in the streets without fear. We didn't have cell phones and were not parked in front of the internet and video games all the time. We roller skated, rode our bikes and didn't make our parents worry about us causing trouble. We were respectful to adults and listened to our parents. I was always close to my mom, and she did so much for me. When my sister and I were little my mom stayed home with us, and my dad worked. From the pictures, my mom's stories and my memories of our younger years, my dad was a lot of fun. I guess I knew from very early on that I wanted to be a mom myself.

I met my husband to be, Bill, in 1990. We met in high school and became good friends. The summer after graduation we were in the same place at the right time and would date for the next eight years until we were married in 1998. We both graduated from Temple University with teaching degrees and headed to Arizona to start our teaching careers and married life.

Leaving our family and friends was not easy, but the opportunities available in Arizona were something we wanted to explore. We both acquired teaching positions immediately and settled in for our first year away from almost everyone we knew. We missed our family and friends, but Arizona was so different from where we grew up with new opportunities for us to explore. We purchased our first new home in Surprise, Arizona even before our first year living away from home was up. We made some wonderful friends at the schools where we taught. A few visits were made back to Pennsylvania, but we knew Arizona was where we would stay.

My dad had recently retired from General Motors after thirty-eight years, and my parents were now looking to move. Being away from both of their daughters would be difficult, and so they made the decision that Arizona would be the place for them. When my parents made the move they lived with us for a few months while waiting for their house to be ready. It was nice having family around again.

Bill and I were expecting our first child in a few months, so it was even more special that his grandparents would be there to greet him. In November of 2001 our amazing son, Quinn was born. He gave us a scare and decided to come out early in an emergency C-section. It was one of the happiest days of our lives when he was born. Quinn was tiny, but perfect. He was the baby we had tried to have for almost a year. Having my parents in Arizona with us was nice, so when in 2001 my sister decided to make the move with her family living here felt complete.

Why Did I Write This Book?

First let me say that I never, in my worst nightmare, would have wanted to write a book on this subject. But because I did have the worst life experience happen to me, I wanted to let people who have never experienced the loss of a child have a better understanding of what life is like for the parents, a sibling, and family members after the passing of a child.

I spent many days so angry I wanted to run until I passed out, punch a wall, scream out loud until I lost my voice-all because I saw someone else enjoying what I had lost. And yes I have done almost all of these things. When I see other parents ignore, yell or set bad examples for their children, I can't help but wonder why don't they understand how precious their children are and take their parenting responsibilities seriously?

I'm not sure parents, friends and family understand how sad it makes the parents who have lost a child feel when they hear them make statements to children such as: " Go play, I don't have time for this right now," "I can't wait until your bedtime," "You are on my nerves." I want to beg them to be more considerate of what they say and to think before they speak,-I want them to appreciate the fact that this child is here with you now, who needs and wants your attention. I see my children as my life, and I work hard every day to be a good parent. Yes, I said my children because even though Quinn is not here with me, he will always be my child.

I also wanted to write this book for my amazing sons, Quinn and Will. Quinn worked hard every day to please people. He was creative and loved to help others. His brother, Will, learned patience and so much kindness from the brother he loved so much. Quinn had sensory processing disorder (SPD).

One month before the accident that took Quinn's life he started a brain training program to help retrain the neurons in his brain. After each week of training, we witnessed Quinn's sensory issues improve. Amazing changes were taking place, and it seemed that all of the challenges Quinn faced were starting to disappear. Other than the medical staff, his dad, brother, grandparents and myself were the only witnesses to see how hard he worked.

Now Quinn is in heaven with my dad, the grandfather who really understood him and his disability. The week we all spent together, the last week of their lives was wonderful. I was so overjoyed for Quinn to be able to accomplish the things he did with so much less of a struggle. I want all to know Quinn was special, and that he is going to make this world a better place for so many children. I hope his foundation, Treasures from Quinn, will help to allow other children who face the same challenges to have a chance for success.

SPD is often misunderstood, and you can learn more about it in Chapter 10. Through his foundation, we hope to help other parents, who can't afford training, the opportunity to show how successful this can be for their child. You can find more information on his web site at TreasuresFromQuinn.com

PART ONE

OUR STORY

CHAPTER 1

The Accident

Quinn in a hot tub full of bubbles!!

Preparing for Vacation

We were all packed up and ready to go on our family vacation in our Chevy Trailblazer. I remember when we bought this truck; it was the end of 2003. We wanted a bigger vehicle so we would have room for more than just the three of us. My parents spent a lot of time with us, and now we would have room for everyone. They watched Quinn so we could go pick up our new

General Motors family vehicle. My dad approved especially because he worked for GM. Friends of ours had purchased a Trailblazer for their family, and not only did we do research on it, but had ridden in it with our child many times. We believed this would be the safe family vehicle for us.

Our boys, now ages five and eight, were so excited to have their grandparents going with us on vacation again. Beach chairs, bikes, toys, food and games all loaded into the truck. My family teased me about how much I packed, but when we needed something 99% of the time I had it.

My mom had just finished radiation therapy. She was battling uterine cancer, and this was her two week break before starting her second round of chemo. It was also good for my dad to get a break from witnessing my mom struggle through her treatments. For the first time in his life he feared he might lose her. A week sitting on the beach with her family relaxing and enjoying the cool sea air was something they needed. My boys knew to treat Mom Mom with care while she was recovering. They were the best medicine for her.

Quinn was working hard with his therapy at the Center for Cognitive Enhancement. We were all so proud of his progress. Will was excited that he would be able to tell everyone about this trip in school, when he started kindergarten the following month. My husband and I enjoyed the extra help with our boys, and my dad enjoyed entertaining them. Walking on the beach, searching for treasures, collecting shells, learning to fish, riding our bikes, and of course getting ice cream were all things my dad told them we could do.

My husband and dad took turns driving. Many funny stories were told along the way. This was the beginning of a trip we would all remember. Time was spent on the beach playing in the sand and collecting treasures. Bike rides, fishing, and of course, ice cream cones were enjoyed. By the end of the week we wished we could have stayed longer. On our last night we enjoyed a sea-food dinner and then headed home in the morning. The boys were excited to see our pups again and tell their friends all about the fun week we all had. We stopped for gas and were closer to home, but we never reached home that day.

Quinn and Pappy fishing in the ocean

July 3, 2010

July 3rd 2010, was the worst day of my life. It is the day a huge part of me died. Bill, our eight-year-old son, Quinn, our five year old son, Will, my mom and dad and I were returning to Arizona after a wonderful week long vacation at the California beach. We were an hour from home, and I can remember hearing a loud noise and my dad yell, "Oh no." A tire on our Chevy Trailblazer SUV blew; we went off the road and rolled several times.

Everything happened so fast, but as it did, it felt like slow motion. I can remember the SUV rolling and dirt and broken glass flying everywhere. I can still feel my arm flying through the window, smashing the glass and being forced back in again as we rolled. I remember saying "Please stop," over and over again. It felt like we would never stop rolling.

For as much debris as hit my face as we rolled, I can't remember feeling that much pain until I was forced to be strapped down and put into the ambulance.

What I saw will haunt me for the rest of my life. I remember the blurry first sights that I saw, and the haunting cries I heard. It was as if I was seeing things in slow motion. I remember seeing my father critically wounded, not making a sound. Then I scanned to my right and saw the left side of my husband, Bill. I could see his leg up on the dashboard and he seemed to be smashed up against the door.

As I listened to Bill attempt to yell for help, I scrambled for my cell phone that happened to be in front of me on the floor in my purse. Somehow I managed to call 911. On the right side of me I saw my mom crushed up against the back seat door. I remember her moaning as I screamed for anyone to help, to call for helicopters. I looked in the back row where my boys were seated. I could hear Will crying, and remember seeing some blood on his hands and arms. Next I discovered a mother's worst nightmare. My eight year old son, Quinn, was not in the car. Total shock kicked in and I managed to get myself out of my seatbelt and through the smashed window where kind people were there to help me get out. In my mind, it all happened so fast. I have no idea how all the people were able to get to us so quickly.

A wonderful man, who I had never met helped get my son Will out of the truck. I was told he stayed with him and, took care of him until the helicopter arrived.

I remember the extreme heat of the desert floor on my bare feet. As I screamed for anyone to take me to my son, I didn't realize that I was bleeding or what my injuries were. People scrambled to find a shoe that was lying on the ground so I could be guided to my other son. I can remember blurting out information about ages, allergies, medications and conditions as if I was a robot programmed to report personal information.

All I wanted was to be with my children. I felt so many emotions as I approached Quinn. I remember the kind people who were there to help were attending to Quinn. I was told that the woman holding his head was a nurse who happened to drive by with her children in the car. She stopped to help Quinn, and I am forever grateful to her. The little time I spent with Quinn before the helicopter took him away is time I will never forget.

Quinn was fighting. He was struggling with all of us as we all tried to keep him still. I can only imagine how much pain he was in, and I felt helpless and wanted him to be free from pain instantly. I wanted the helicopter to be there waiting to give him pain meds and take him to the hospital to have his broken leg fixed.

I also wanted to get into the helicopter to tell the paramedics about Quinn, about why he didn't deserve a second of pain and about the amazing boy he was. I know that he knew I was there, but I never got to hear his sweet voice again. As I held his hand, he pulled it up to his mouth, and bit down on my fingers. I know he wanted to tell me something, and I begged for him to keep his amazing blue eyes open, and to stay awake.

I wanted to go with him in the helicopter, but they would not let me. I rattled off a list of things about Quinn and begged the EMT's to please take care of my son. I needed them to know about his sensory issues, and I just wanted to get to the hospital with the rest of my family so I could have some control.

As the EMT's directed me to lie down on a stretcher, again, I begged for them to take me to Will. They agreed, but only if I would get strapped down after I saw him. Will was lying on a stretcher on the ground under an umbrella that a kind passerby brought to shade him. He was terrified. The paramedics worked on trying to get an IV in him, and I explained to him the nice people were going to take good care of him, and to be a good boy. I told him I loved him, and would see him soon.

I remember looking to the right as a paramedic asked me some questions about my father. I saw him on the ground covered by a yellow, propped-up tarp. They were doing their best to see if they could save him, but I knew in the back of my mind after what I saw, that my dad was gone.

I couldn't process the conditions of my parents, or husband at the time. I just needed to get to the hospital to see my boys. After the helicopters took off, I tried to make my way to my husband, but the paramedics made me lay back on the stretcher. At this point I could barely see out of my swollen eyes and face.

The next tortuous forty-five minutes in the ambulance felt like hours. I can remember asking repeatedly about my children. They couldn't tell me anything. I begged for the girls in the ambulance to use my cell phone. At some point I made a call to my sister, Donna. Much later we would have a conversation about that call.

I don't think anyone could be prepared for what Donna would see when she arrived at the hospital. She told me during the phone call that my voice was very calm, as I explained that we had been in a bad accident and had broken bones, and the situation was very bad so she needed to get to the hospital right away. Between the neck brace, my limited vision and not being able to move my left arm, I went through what I would call mini panic attacks. I felt trapped, almost paralyzed from being strapped down. My mind raced and besides the pain I felt, every time I struggled to move, all I could concentrate on was getting to the hospital to see my boys.

As I lay in the emergency room alone and full of drugs, pain still racked my body. I begged everyone who came by to please check on my children. I remember feeling so alone, and it felt like hours had passed. The next thing I heard was my husband being brought in. He was yelling in pain. It's hard not to want to communicate when you hear someone you love yelling in pain.

We were told not to talk to each other as they were trying to work on our injuries. I felt even more trapped and suffocated by the restrictive neck brace and the loss of vision from my swelling eyes. All I could do was lay there, listen and wait. I guess they put us out, because the next thing I knew, I was in a dark hospital room by myself. I don't remember any of the scans and other tests they did before I was taken to my room.

That night was very long. I struggled to get any nurses attention who walked by so I could get information about my family. I remember asking over and over again about my family, and for my cell phone. I told them to call my sister, because she would know how everyone was. I had no idea she was already at the hospital, and had already taken over the power of attorney of my entire family. She had been with both of my sons, and was busy making medical decisions about treatments and surgeries for our family.

It wasn't until early the next morning, after consistently asking about my family, did I get the news. Outside in the hall I heard many voices, and I recognized my sister's voice. My sister and brother-in-law came in to my room along with a few staff members. I could see in her eyes that she had to tell me something that a mom should never hear. I told her what I thought she had to tell me, "Dad is gone, right?"

The tears started to flow and she slowly began to tell me that she had been with my son, and how peaceful he looked. Uncontrollable. This is the only way I can describe the emotions and pain I felt. It was if nothing was real. I remember looking around the room and seeing the faces and hearing uncontrollable sadness. It was the day the old me died.

The Trailblazer

Therapy

When we all got home, we knew we needed to find someone to help us cope with our nightmare, but how do you find a therapist? We had no idea, and never thought we would need a grief therapist. Looking for a grief therapist that insurance companies cover isn't an easy task. We discovered many therapists don't accept insurance, and paying privately can become expensive. Not only was it something I had no desire to do, but finding one, and getting an appointment was a challenge. We were grieving parents, who just lost their eight-year-old son. We didn't want to get out of bed, and certainly didn't have the energy to talk to insurance companies to find a therapist. Our first experience with therapy after the accident was not the right fit for us. This therapist didn't have much experience with grief therapy, and after one appointment we knew we would not to go back. We didn't know where to look, so when a couple came to our home who had experienced the painful loss of their daughter, Hannah, they shared some advice.

As I glanced at the mother and her perfectly groomed appearance, I thought how good she looked in comparison to me. I sat there in shorts and a t-shirt with no makeup, dark circles under my eyes, and unbrushed hair. I remember sitting on the couch wondering how they could speak so open about what they experienced, and where they were at that point in their grief. This couple took turns telling us how important it was for them to talk with a therapist. They found a good therapist willing to come to their home after the death of their daughter. Listening to them talk about how they functioned and survived in the first few months after their loss, I felt the littlest bit of hope people could survive the death of their child.

They gave us good advice on being kind to ourselves, and to each other. They shared stories of how they grieved differently, and how they learned to respect each other when they were in different stages of their grief. By the end of their visit, we watched them cry, and even smile a little. They gave us some hope, and we called the therapist.

We were fortunate that this therapist came to our home for the next year to meet with us. We didn't have to leave the house, and we were in our own environment where nobody would see us. What this year of therapy gave me most was a place to dump all my sadness and just talk about missing my son. The therapist was very good at listening to any story I told about Quinn, and encouraged me to speak. He couldn't give me the answer to the question, *why did this happen?* I would learn over the next four years of therapy that no one could answer that question.

After almost a year of therapy at home, new feelings began to surface. My husband and I felt like we had shared enough with this therapist, and were no longer getting the guidance and feedback from him to help us move forward, so we began to see a new therapist. It was difficult to retell her our story from the beginning, but her expertise in grief and trauma therapy was what we needed. She not only looked at us as grieving parents, but as a married couple. The therapy she provided was not something defined in a textbook. Sure we discussed the stages of grief, but there is no real set order to grieve. She listened, sympathized, gave advice and followed through. Over the years she became a friend, and then more like a part of our family. She gave us suggestions on how to survive through the times when grief was so heavy we were ready to give up. She reminded us that we were still needed by many, especially our son, Will. She gave us a reason to lean on each other, but also the ability to recognize the times when we needed to grieve differently.

Therapy was not only needed for us, but for our son, Will. Will was almost six at the time of the accident, and obviously children process things differently than adults. We were advised to look for signs that he may need to talk to a therapist. We invited Will to join us with our in-home therapist, but he wasn't interested in talking much. So we watched, and took note of his emotions. Curiosity, confusion, sadness, blame and anger all surfaced, and we decided he needed a grief therapist.

Will was not comfortable going to therapy alone, so we joined the sessions. Some days he would talk a little, some days not at all. From both our therapy and our son's therapy experience, we realized that paying for and finding the right therapist was worth every penny. The wonderful therapist my husband and I were seeing suggested a children's grief therapist she trusted. We met with her first, and discussed our concerns.

Ana included us in some of the sessions, but as time went on, we were only invited in at the end of the session. It was hard for me not being present to see all that Will was working through. Ana used many different types of therapy with Will, including drawing, story writing and sand art. After a few months, we noticed Will was managing his anger and grief better. His feelings didn't disappear, but he now had tools to use as a way to deal with his grief.

Will's therapy sessions eventually went from twice a week to once a month. As Will matured over the next two-and-a-half years, he processed his trauma and loss differently. He returned to therapy many times to help manage his grief that surfaced on occasion.

EMDR Therapy

At the scene of the accident even though I had limited vision, I was there on the ground with Quinn before he was taken away. The images and memories of that time were so vivid that I was unable to lie down without remembering the sounds, images, and physical pain just like it was happening all over again. Even the motion of being on the ground and leaning over sent my mind spinning out of control- right back to the scene of the accident. I was unable to sleep lying down, so when I was able to rest, I slept upright. Again and again, my mind would become fixated and frozen, and I'd remember the trauma as badly as if I had gone through it the first time.

When I told my therapist that I was reliving a traumatic scene from the accident over and over in my head, she suggested a treatment called EMDR that might help me. EMDR is eye movement desensitization and reprocessing therapy. This type of therapy uses an approach that has been effective for the treatment of trauma, so after a short discussion about EMDR, I was willing to try it.

The goal of this therapy for me was to process my painful memories and replace them with a new memory. Whenever I was reminded of the trauma, the images continued to be triggered. When I processed the memories, I didn't have to explain the disturbing memories in detail. I described the scene by telling where we were and why I felt so helpless. While briefly concentrating on the most painful memory in my mind, I tracked my therapist's finger movements by going back-and-forth with my eyes. With EMDR treatments, I still remembered what happened, but after many sessions it became less upsetting. I am a true believer in this type of therapy, and think it was an important treatment for this part of my trauma.

When things became more difficult for Will, we took him to

see a wonderful woman named Ana, who was recommended as an excellent children's therapist. After meeting with us first, she welcomed Will into her office. By no means is Will a shy person, and as parents, we thought him to be mature well beyond his years. The little boy we began to see displaying aggressive verbal and physical behavior was one we didn't know. Besides his sadness over the loss of his brother and grandfather, he had angry feelings toward God, and especially the people responsible for their deaths. He wanted someone to blame, and anyone associated with "taking his brother away from him," was bad. He associated any GM employee as one of the bad people responsible, and complained about how anyone could still be driving a GM vehicle.

EMDR is also used to help children recover from traumas that have happened in their lives. After getting to know Will better, Ana discussed introducing EMDR therapy. In children EMDR can be administered by eye movement, tapping hands back and forth on knees or legs, or even using sounds and music from one ear to another. Ana explained when traumatic events happen, our brain has a difficult time putting all the different pieces together. When something someone said or did, or something Will saw or even smelled brought up a bad memory, he found himself having emotions he never expressed before. Ana used EMDR therapy with Will to replace some confusing and bad feelings that he was keeping around and made room for good memories.

We believed the EMDR therapy in combination with many other types of therapy Ana used with Will, helped him to express his feelings without so much anger, and in a healthier way. Will continued to see Ana for therapy until we felt he showed enough progress to take a break. As parents we saw many changes in Will, and so we gave him the option. We talked with Will about letting us know if and when he needed to visit Ana again. Will did take a break for a while, but has been back to therapy on and off when feelings and memories become too difficult.

I Joined a New Team

I am now with a team nobody wants to join. Friends want to help, but they know life as it once was lived. For me I couldn't live my old life. I died the day I lost my son. The thought of laughter sounded ridiculous, and I had no desire to do the things I did with my friends in the past. No shopping, pedicures, dinner, movies, barbeques, holiday get togethers or birthday celebrations. Everyone connected to my life before the accident still had their family. Their lives would go on. As much as some tried, they would never feel the hell I had to live in because they hadn't lost what I lost.

I never asked to be on this team, and I wish I could quit. By quitting I mean leaving this world to be in heaven with my sweet son again. Why must I stay on this team? My answer is that I must live for my surviving son and husband.

That doesn't mean a grieving parent wants to hear you say, "Be happy that you have another child." I live another day each day because of my son and husband who survived. The way I feel now is that I don't think I will ever have another great day. Some days will be good, but those days my husband and I owe to our son Will. He picks us up when we are feeling low and makes us appreciate him more than we ever have before.

Unfortunately, there are some others who like me are on my team. I found a measure of peace when meeting with another mom, who also lives with the misery of losing a child. We connected with another family, who lost their young daughter to a careless driver. I met this mom at a fundraising event held in honor of her daughter, Ellie. I attended this event, because I identified with her situation, and wanted to show support.

It was the first time I went out to an event since I lost my son. A good friend sent me an email about this benefit, and thought I could meet someone who would understand some of the same pain I was feeling. I am grateful to my friend, because this mom who was forced to be on the same team of loss, is now one of my dearest friends.

I remember not being able to speak as the tears ran down my face on the day I met Taunya. She knew how devastated I was, and I felt how fresh her pain was even thought only two years had passed since she lost her daughter. She was someone who understood what I was going through. We began to meet often to share memories of our amazing children, and in the process we were making new happy memories. Our children share the same feelings of loss of a sibling, and have a friendship in which they understand each other.

Our families continue to get together and find comfort in our "new normal." Holidays, birthdays, accident anniversaries, and the days we lost our precious children are difficult days for us. Holidays are, of course, times for families to get together to celebrate, but for us the idea of celebrating without our loved ones did not feel right. On our team, we see the day of a holiday as another day without our children. What were once days filled with excitement and family fun, will always be tainted by the sadness for who we lost. As parents we want our children to experience life, and make many memories. So as much as we want to stay in bed during many of these days, we do what we can for our surviving children. They never asked for this life, and we will continue to try to let them experience as "normal" of a life as they possibly can.

CHAPTER 2

The First Year

My journal

The One Year Anniversary

I don't think it should be called the anniversary. To me anniversary means celebrating the day my husband and I got married and began our future together as the first two in our family. Every year for eleven years we celebrated that day. We lost our son fifteen days before our twelfth year wedding anniversary. There was no celebrating; it was another hard and long day.

In August, Will started school. What should have been a very exciting time for both of our boys was tainted with sadness. Quinn could not be the big brother showing Will the ropes of elementary school. Taking a picture of Will on his first day brought back flashes of Quinn's first day. I did my best to turn away, breathe deeply and quickly wipe the tears away before turning back around to force a smile at Will. This was supposed to be an awesome beginning to a new chapter in all of our lives.

October came, my birthday passed with little recognition- as that was my wish. Will's sixth birthday quickly followed. Birthday parties had been my specialty. I'd make homemade cakes shaped and decorated into my boys' favorite theme of the year. Handmade favors and games, and good old-fashioned family fun. I just couldn't do it anymore. I rented a session of jumping at a party place, and somehow made it through the day. I have no idea how I was able to do it, but with Will's persuasion, I did buy a store- made cake and decorate it for him. I look back at the pictures friends took and can see the sparks missing from our faces.

It was recommended to us to journal our thoughts and feelings. Here is my first journal entry:

I want to be writing your name on a piece of paper from school, or on your new school supplies. I bought this journal because it is green. You loved the color green, and anytime I see green I think of you. I know you would say "that's nice Mom," and you would probably want the smooth green ribbon in the book for one of your treasures, and you know I would give it to you. There isn't anything I wouldn't do for you. I love you every second of the day. I don't keep track of the days, but I know that I keep waiting to see you come downstairs in the morning. I miss how you would smile at me and hug me good morning. I want to feel your hug again so much it takes my breath away. I don't care so much about myself, and I don't look very good. I could always count on you even when I didn't look or feel my best, you would say "You look great Mom." That's my Quinn, you always wanted to please me, and YOU DID. I love you so much. There are things I want to say to you. I only wanted you to be happy and safe. These things don't happen to a family like ours. We went to your favorite place and got to spend time with Mom Mom and Pappy. Mom Mom needed time to get better and you were taking great care of her. Pappy searched for treasures with you and went fishing in the ocean. We all went to Lego Land and you were amazing there. We couldn't be more proud of your patience and manners. I have great pictures of us that I thought everyone would be happy to see. I never want you to think because I am so sad that I don't love you, but life is never the same. On the day you were taken away from me I died too. I wish we all died with you that day. Dad and Will miss you. I am trying to be a good mom to Will, but I was supposed to be a mom to my two boys, not just one. I wish we could all be together. Things are hard to do. I am angry and sad, numb and quiet. I know it would break your heart to see me this way, and I hope you can't. Your pictures are all over, and I just want one more hug. I don't know how to live again. I don't know how to go to the place we all loved (the beach) I can still see you playing in the sand with your brother. I can feel you holding my hand when I took you to the shops by the harbor. It was just us and you told me "I love you Mom, you're the best Mom in the world."

I feel like my life is in slow motion. I can feel heavy weights on my shoulders. Walking at times is hard- my legs get very heavy. I can't be the person I was, I want to hide and run. I don't want to reward myself or go out and talk to people. I feel so alone. I know I have your dad and Will, but you completed our family.

I can remember how sad I was when I couldn't get pregnant. But the day we found out you were in my belly I was the happiest person alive. I was so careful, and did everything right for you. Dad was so scared when the doctor called him at work and told him to come to the hospital. You wanted to come out early. You were so tiny and amazing. I never wanted to let you go. I knew everything about you, and we would only leave you with Mom Mom and Pappy if we had to go out. I couldn't wait to hold you as soon as we rushed back. Everyone thought I was crazy because I had them write down everything you did so I wouldn't miss a thing. I never wanted to miss anything you did. Now I don't know what to do. My job was to take care of you and be a mom. I needed you as much as you needed me.

On our first Halloween without Quinn, we took Will to a neighborhood we had never been to where nobody knew us. Will had just turned six, and we couldn't cancel Halloween, so we wandered from house to house like zombies doing our best to let Will experience the night as he should have.

Next Quinn's birthday arrived, and I can't describe in words how distraught I was. There was no party to plan, no presents to buy, and no cake to make, so we wrote messages on green balloons and sent them up into the air.

Thanksgiving was spent away at a resort being busy with

swimming and other activities other than recognizing anything to do with the day. Somehow we survived, but now Christmas was next, and for me it was a day filled with reoccurring torture.

Journal Entry –

Thanksgiving 2010

We are not thankful this year. We are not celebrating. This was a special day for our family to all be together. We are not together, and I can't bear to sit at a table without you and Pappy with us. We are leaving the house. Just me, Will and dad going to a hotel. No turkey dinner, no being with our family. Just a few days to get through wishing things were not this way. I so enjoyed the way you would help set the table, and make special things for everyone. You loved turkey and mashed potatoes with lots of gravy. We ate a little fast food on Thanksgiving. It was sad; we were the only three people in the place. Dad and I stayed up late reading and staring into space. I don't know why we read? There are no answers. We wish for the impossible.

You would have had ice cream for dessert. I can picture how happy you would be playing with your brother and cousins, Pappy would be playing games with you too. There was no turkey, ice cream or pie. No Asti toast with Aunt Donna and Mom Mom. I have no desire. I want you here to complete our family. I love you so much.

Christmas morning came and yes, Santa had delivered gifts for Will, but there was no ignoring the sadness of Quinn's absence. I never knew I could cry with such force that I felt like I was suffocating while drenching myself with tears. All we knew for eight years was living as a family of three and then four when Will came along. Now we are back to three, and Quinn's absence makes everything feel incomplete. We look at life as if we have had two lives. One that we lived before Quinn died and the one we have now.

Some may think that since it's been a year, we should start moving on. I am still amazed at how I lived through my first six months without Quinn. I am now realizing that I was numb for part of the first year. So much of my time was spent in disbelief and numbing my mind with books, looking for the answer to my question, "Why did this happen?"

Even though it felt like a year had passed, it had only been six months since this nightmare began in July. January arrived and it was now a new year. February, March and April were all filled with family birthdays. Again, any holiday was difficult, and we didn't feel up to celebrating. School was out in May, and we would have two more months before the dreadful day in July would arrive. Starting July third we would now have to experience for the second time every day without our son. It was bad enough the first time doing everything without him in our lives, so imagine reliving life with his absence all over again.

We still get the question, "How are you?" I sometimes say ok, but mostly I mumble out a groan or shake my head. I wish people would just say hello, or give me a hug and tell me they think about us every day.

I Lost My Full Time Job

When my husband and I moved to Arizona in 1998, I began my first permanent teaching job. I graduated from Temple University with an art education teaching degree, and was very excited to start teaching art.

After Quinn was born in 2001, I continued teaching, but had a hard time leaving my son. He was in the best hands with my parents and a close family friend who watched him while I was at school, but I always couldn't wait for the day to be over and pick him up. As soon as the school day was over, I rushed to get Quinn and couldn't wait to hear all about his day. When my second son, Will was born in 2004, I think I knew the day I met him that my boys would be my new job. As much as I enjoyed teaching art, I wanted to be a full time mom to my boys. It was decided that my teaching career would be put on hold. To this day, I have to say that I made the right choice.

When people would ask me what I did for a living, I would say, "I'm a mom." Quinn and Will were my full time job. I had the best job in the world. Every minute of my day revolved around my boys' schedules. From the time they got up in the morning until they fell asleep at night, and many times in the middle of the night, I was there to take care of them. When I lost my eight-year-old son, I lost my full time job. Yes, I still have my lovable son, Will. Now I will continue to be the best mom I can for my surviving son.

No two children are going to be the same, have the same personalities, needs and wants. Quinn was special in so many ways. Quinn had sensory processing disorder. He required a lot of support from me and his dad. If you do not know what sensory processing disorder is, I will explain it in chapter 10.

When I lost Quinn, too many parts of each day and week became empty. My job as a mom changed forever, and I felt so incomplete. I was no longer responsible for helping Quinn with his struggles in school, to find the right solution to his sensory issues, or to take him to occupational therapy. No one understood Quinn like I did. I worked very hard to help find solutions to his challenges, so he could succeed just as any other child could. Will would soon be entering kindergarten, and Quinn should have been entering third grade. I was no longer needed to do all the things my "full time job" required me to do. I was left with so much emptiness that it made me question even more why I was still here.

My Dad

Inot only lost my son in the accident, but I lost my dad. Therapists, counselors and the many books I have read say that you can really only mourn one loss at a time. I don't think I will ever stop mourning my son, so I wonder when will I have time to mourn my dad? I was consumed with constant grief at the loss of my son. I thought about my dad, but I didn't have enough energy to process losing him too.

When the horrific accident happened, I went into shock. I saw my dad, and I think I knew he wasn't going to survive. My motherly instincts automatically kicked in, and all I could do was worry about my boys; all I could do was try to get to my boys.

I can remember the paramedics asking me questions about my dad. I rambled facts about his birthdate and allergies. I was in what I would call robot mode-a-dreamlike state. At the time, I could not process how serious and how devastating it all was. Now I have the rest of my life to process it, and I have to say that I do every day.

My dad served in the Navy, and was always a proud American. He worked for General Motors in Trenton New Jersey. When my sister and I were very young he worked many different shifts and often worked overtime on the weekends.

My father took our family to the General Motors plant in the early 1980's to learn about vehicle safety. We listened to people speak, and watched very graphic films about the dangers of not wearing seatbelts. From that day forward, we never drove in a vehicle without our seatbelts. He was loyal to this company, and supported GM in many ways. "Buy American, support the company I work for," was something he said on a regular basis. All of the vehicles in our family were GM vehicles.

I remember when I was dating my future husband, and he came over with his new Toyota truck. My dad came outside, and the first thing he said was, "You're not parking that thing in my driveway. That's not a GM vehicle." As much as he liked Bill, he never approved of his choice in purchasing that truck.

A few times I have spotted someone in a store who looks like my dad, and it tricks my mind into thinking it's him. I get a quick rush and want to yell out, "Hey Dad!", but then in a few seconds reality hits. Something like this is enough of a reminder of what I lost, and it makes me feel low for the rest of the day. My life was forever changed that painful day in July in a way that not only killed my father and my son, it took away who I was.

My nephew, Nathan, was born in June of 2000, and he decided that my dad would be called Pappy. Quinn was born next, followed by my other nephew, Nick, and then Will. Everyone called my dad Pappy. Maybe the name stuck since most of the time he was surrounded by his grandchildren. Because my dad was such a big part of our lives, it is difficult to not miss his presence.

Losing my dad means no more complete family celebrations. There will always be the empty space where he used to sit on the couch, at the table, and under the waterfall where he liked to sit in our pool. These are the images that make me grieve for him. It is miserable, and these thoughts torment me because I know that he wouldn't want me to be sad.

Despite not driving a GM vehicle, my husband had a good friendship with my dad and also misses him. They enjoyed doing many things together, and I believe Bill was like the son Dad never had. Bill became part of our family over the eight years we dated before we got married. Fishing, watching football, playing cards, doing home repairs, and getting a bargain at a yard sale were all things they shared and often did together. My dad influenced Bill in many ways and vice versa. That was especially good for my dad.

Like most dads, my dad had some funny and annoying quirks. We remember how much he disliked it when someone left the front door open or forgot to shut off the lights and television when nobody was in the room. This drove him crazy. I can still hear his voice when the refrigerator door was open too long, or when he made us unplug everything during a thunderstorm so it wouldn't blow up. Yes, we knew money didn't grow on trees, and even though he said it we weren't letting all the cold air out of the house by opening the front door for more than five seconds.

On better days we can now look up and taunt him by standing with the fridge open, or leaving that light on and hope he is laughing at us. Sometimes we wonder if he will send some lightning our way to knock out our television as punishment. Even though we poke fun at these quirks, we have all learned a lot from my dad and often use the *Pappy Method* and *Pappy Advice* to get things done.

My parents with all four boys at the Phoenix zoo

My Mom

When my sister and I were born, my mom stayed home to care for us. She made a lot of sacrifices to be there and give us the things we wanted. She was involved in our school life by volunteering and serving on committees at our school. She helped with our girl scout troupes, supported our dance classes, and after school sports. She always saved money so we could be involved in the activities we enjoyed. We were very fortunate to have a mom who encouraged us to be active and learn new things.

I lived at home until I got married and moved to Arizona. Going away to college was not for me, because I was comfortable at home, and enjoyed having my own room and quiet places to do my work. I stayed at home and commuted into the city to attend Temple University. I never thought I would move away from my family, but Arizona had opportunities I couldn't pass up. With my parents moving to Arizona in 2001, I didn't have to wait long to be with family once again.

My mom and Quinn

Sundays were fun for us. My mom and I did our own thing while Dad and my husband watched football. When Quinn was born, my mom was there to help, and even though I was now a mom myself, it was still nice having her around. It may seem unusual to some, but our relationship had been this way for all of my life, and I just assumed things would stay constant. Due to the accident, change did happen, and I believe the losses we suffered upset our relationship in many ways.

Even though my mom and I both survived the accident, our world changed. She was still the great mom she had always been before this nightmare, but I am a different person now. My personality and ability to communicate were forever altered the day of the crash.

Before the accident, my mom and I would talk about my children and everything that was going on in our family life. We went shopping, got pedicures, and took family vacations together. My mom and dad attended almost every school event, holiday and birthday for my children. They were a part of our everyday lives. After the accident, I felt like I couldn't talk about Quinn without sobbing. It was just too painful.

Journal Entry –

Gardening brought me so much joy. I think I loved it because Mom Mom was always excited about it when I was a little girl. Maybe that's why you loved it so much. I wanted to think you got that from me. Now I don't enjoy our garden. I haven't planted any new vegetables, and it looks so empty. I want you to be here digging for worms and making dams. The shovel you were digging with the last time we were in the garden is still pushed into the soil. That is where it will stay. Because I can't share it with you it doesn't seem worth doing. The only planting has been your seeds. (We had a picture of Quinn put on seed packets, and they were mailed out to friends and family.) *I will take good care of them and hope they grow into beautiful amazing flowers. I hope you and Pappy can look down from heaven and see them. We put another pot near yours with Pappy's seeds in it. You were very special to Pappy and he loves you very much.*

While my other son was making new memories, I was devastated, knowing that I wouldn't have any new memories of Quinn. My mom loved my boys, but they were her grandchildren. She wouldn't be missing all the special moments and accomplishments only I as a mom would miss. I don't think there were any right things she or anyone could have said to me. But a mom wants to fix everything and this was one thing nobody could fix.

My mom continues to be there for whatever we need, but in our new life, (the life we never asked for) I see things differently. We don't have the same happy, loving family relationship we all had in the past, and we don't have the same energy we had when we were all together before the accident. We now live for our surviving son and use all of our energy to make sure he lives a comfortable and happy life- as he deserves. Every loss is devastating, but the loss of a child, in my opinion, is the worst loss of all.

During the first year after the accident we were all consumed with our own type of grief. We didn't focus on family dinners, birthdays and events. We were all trying to figure out this new life. My contact was limited with almost everyone. My mom spent most of that year recovering from her injuries and learning how to live alone for the first time. I could not be the one to comfort her, because I couldn't find comfort for myself. I was trying to figure out how to get through another day.

It was painful just to walk into my parent's house. This was the house that was once filled with a family making memories. Now it seemed so empty and quiet. I could not sit and grieve with my mom. I don't know why, but I guess I knew this was a wound even a mom couldn't fix.

As months and years passed, little by little, we communicated more with my mom. My mom was Wills only living grandparent in the state, and I wanted her to be a part of his life. My husband and I had decided not to spend the traditional holidays as we had in the past, but as time went on, we've done more together.

About two and a half years after the accident, another event distracted my grieving process in an unwelcomed way. After a surgery-gone-wrong from complications, my mom began a yearlong hospital stay from which she is still recovering. My life was put on hold and my focus turned to protecting my mother. I was consumed with her fight to live and her recovery process.

I don't know if I was too busy to deal with my own life, or if this distraction put most of my grief on hold. I don't know how I had the strength to go to the hospital most days and nights to sit, talk, help with grooming, and give my mom hope to keep fighting. Being constantly busy, and not have much time to stop and slow down to think of how much I missed my old life, I found was both good and bad. Good because I had a purpose and some control over decisions that could save my mom's life; and bad because when being in charge slowed down, as my mom stayed on the path to recovery, my everyday reality hit me once again. Mom had her own challenges ahead, and I was there to help, but I was dealing with my own issues too. I hadn't figured out how to get back to my new normal, and my mom was just learning what her new normal was going to be.

Slowly time moves on. Many things aren't easier to do, they are just different. Now Mom has us over for dinner, and we invite her to our home. She attends school events for Will and has helped out in his classroom. My husband is great at helping out with most of the things my dad used to do at their house. My son, Will, enjoys spending time with his grandmother, and talks openly with her about my dad and Quinn.

I am proud of her. She has overcome so much, and is learning how to live again. Shopping, helping with all of her grandchildren, traveling to see her family back East, and being involved with her group of friends keeps her busy.

My Sister, Donna

Donna was the first born, and I came along a little over two years later. My parents told us many stories about the sister relationship we shared from infant stage through our early teen years. Donna was a very protective, big sister. I remember my mom telling me that she always wanted to help with her baby sister. They sometimes called her "Donna Do," because she often said, "Donna Do," when she wanted to do something. Who will push the stroller, who will hold the baby, who will dress and feed the baby? "Donna Do," she'd reply.

She let people know she had a sister and many times it benefitted her more. Weekly Friday night trips to the bank included asking the teller for a lollypop for her sister, even though I was too little to have one. In elementary school she was there to pick me up from my classroom to ride the bus home. In middle school, she was there to show me the ropes, and give me advice. In high school, I had the advantage of knowing a senior, and not being teased and pushed around as the incoming sophomores sometimes were.

As we grew up even though we had different personalities, we shared many interests. Babysitting together, working at the same pizza shop, bakery and clothing boutique were all jobs we shared. We studied dance for many years, took ceramic classes, and managed baseball teams in high school. She was there to help me finish many papers late at night before she went away for College.

We shared many interests, but we had many differences. I was comfortable being at home, while Donna couldn't wait to go away to college. She majored in business, and I studied art education. She lived at school with roommates, while I lived at home, and commuted to college. Donna enjoyed the freedom, independent, and sometimes party life that living on a college campus offered. I, on the other hand, preferred my own quiet space to work, sleep, and to have my friends nearby. I remember going up to Millersville to visit her. After that trip, I knew dorm life was not for me. Tiny rooms, a community bathroom, no kitchen, not being able to have a space to work other than the library, and the constant noise of people running and yelling in the hallways to much for me. I needed to be able to work on my own schedule, and not have the distractions dorm life came with.

After college, my sister got a job in the city. Soon after, she got engaged, and bought a house in Ridley Park, Pennsylvania. She was a short half hour drive away, and many weekends were spent staying at her home. Her future husband, Joe got along great with my future husband, Bill, and we often spent weekends, holidays and vacations with them.

Moving away to Arizona in 1998 left us missing our families, but jobs, affordable housing, and no more snowy winters were enough reasons to give it a try. Bill and I made a few trips back to Pennsylvania, and Donna and Joe came to visit us in Arizona. We stayed in contact by telephone almost every day, but we had different ideas about where we wanted to live.

When my nephew, Nathan, was born in 2000, it wasn't easy being so far away. Again a few trips were made to visit, but now I had another family member to miss- my nephew.

September 11, 2001 is a day the word will never forget. When the attacks happened, it was a day that threatened the lives of some of my family members who were working in New York and Philadelphia. My sister was one of them. This tragic attack convinced my sister that she and her family should be closer to us. My parents were already living with us in Arizona, and finding out that we would all be together again was something I never thought would happen. I was so happy!

Before another full year had passed, we were all now residents of the state of Arizona. Holidays, birthdays, and most weekends were spent all together as a family once again. With my parents living a short two miles from my sister and her family, we decided to make the move from Surprise to their part of town. After our move we were all within a two mile radius of each other. We were all together, with children of our own, who could now enjoy growing up with grandparents, aunts, uncles and cousins.

Fast forward to June 25, 2010. We were all over at my sister's house celebrating her son Nathan's birthday. We all got together for dinner, cake and present's the night before we left for vacation. None of us could have ever imagined it would be the last family birthday celebration we would have with Quinn and my dad.

Nothing would ever be the same again. My sister got the call on July 3rd. I don't know how, but I told her to come to the hospital. When she arrived, she was met with hospital staff, who informed her of the deaths of our father, and my son-her nephew, Quinn. I had no idea of most of the events that took place that night until much later.

Donna took over as Power of Attorney, and had to make all medical decisions for each member of our family. She had to inform the rest of our family, friends, neighbors and employers. She made arrangements to take time off of work so she could help care for us when we got out of the hospital. She did something I couldn't even think about; she made the funeral arrangements.

As the word spread, she took on the job of sending out an email chain to keep everyone informed. She posted updates about our progress, and spoke for us as we were unable to see or speak to anyone.

At that time, I didn't want to get out of bed, eat, shop, pay the bills, clean the house or take care of the dogs. Donna made arrangements with all the people who were waiting to help to take care of everything. Her husband, Joe, read all the medical bills that came in, consulted with the insurance companies, and left us a note to write a check. He also dealt with the devastating task of retrieving personal items from our vehicle. I couldn't think about how this was affecting her family. I know they were constantly busy dealing with everything, including managing my mom's care. They didn't have time to think or completely fall apart. Someone had to do these tasks, and we were numb and barely functioning ourselves.

Later in August, Will and my nephews started school. Donna

was back to work, and we were homebound, still trying to learn how to function. She enjoyed her job, and she needed to get back to doing what she loved. My job at the time was being a full time mom to my boys. I no longer felt like I could do my job. August 26, was a big birthday for my sister, but it passed without any celebrating from us. October birthdays passed, Quinn's November birthday passed, and then Thanksgiving arrived. I know my sister wanted to keep things as normal as possible for her boys, but I couldn't do the family get together. Christmas consisted of a short visit with gifts for Will, and I appreciated that they respected the fact that we were not able to celebrate.

Our relationship changed over the next few years, not because I loved her any less, but because I was a different person, and I saw life differently. I missed my old life, and, like her, I wished I could return to my old "normal life," but there would be nothing normal about our family again. I imagined her having bad days when the reality of her losses resurfaced.

For me, every day was a bad day. I know she wished I could show some of the "old me," but that person was gone. I wasn't trying to punish her, or her family, but just the thought of walking into her home without my complete family devastated me. Everywhere I looked, I missed seeing Quinn. Too many memories were made there, and it was mentally and physically painful not to see my son there.

I do my best to be present for my nephews when I can. Donna does the same for Will. As my nephews grow older, they don't have as much in common with Will. He remains without his brother, and they continue to grow up. Life will go on, and things will continue to be different.

Where are My Friends?

I lost my son and dad, but I also lost some of my friends and family in a different way. I don't blame some of my friends for falling off the radar after a few months. To most people who have not experienced the loss of a child, a few months may seem like a lot of time to grieve for a loss. If you think so then without a doubt, you truly don't understand what it is like to lose a child. Everything is forever changed.

Every milestone, every school event, sporting event, birthday, holiday, every dinner without the child that you once shared is foreign and different in a disturbing way. Imagine sitting down to dinner and looking at an empty chair that was once filled with your child. This is what our family of three now sees every time we sit down to eat. At every school event I wonder what Quinn's projects would have looked like, and I miss seeing how proud he was to show us his work.

Journal Entry –

Another school function tonight. These are difficult for me. I go because Will should not be deprived and he hears about it in school, so why should he not be included. Hell describes my night. Sobbing and seeing people I have not seen, seeing their faces and sadness. This sucks! I feel exhausted and done. Another thing we do for Will. It should be exciting and fun. I can't do it. I do what I can for Will. Every bit of strength is for him. He needs to have a normal and better than normal childhood if possible. He has had to go through and continues to go through this new life he never asked for.

It is difficult to see parents and their children who were my son's classmates. I mostly see sadness in their faces as they walk by, but

43

very few stop to say they are thinking about us. Most people don't know what to say, so they say nothing.

Pay attention to body language. If you can see that the grieving parent is upset and crying, it might not be a good time to go over and start a conversation. But when a friend would come over and just say even a few sentences then be on their way, it showed me that they were still there.

I considered myself a friendly, compassionate, helpful and outgoing person. I feel like I was punished in so many ways, because I lost my dad and son. I was the mom who tried to make everyone feel welcome and helped to see that everyone was included.

Now I often hide in the shadows feeling the pain of what I don't have. I was a person who got together to laugh with friends. The past we shared is filled with memories of my old life, the life I want back. The problem is I can't have my old life back, and being with old friends makes me realize what I am missing. Learning to live with the pain of losing a child won't ever go away, but as time passes we all have to learn to live with it.

Journal Entry –

Claudia came today. I finally let her come to see me. She is a great person. She loves us all. She is a great mom and friend. She let me cry, she listened, she was strong, she cried, she understands. She is sad for us. She has two children and she can't imagine how it would feel if she lost one. She tries. She says she won't go away. She says "I will listen."

As a friend you will have to make the decision to wait around until the grieving parents are ready. I see people I know almost everywhere I go. Some smile and wave, some give a passing hug, and some look the other way. My advice is to not go away. If you care you won't go away no matter how long it may take the grieving family members to attempt to restart their life again. An e mail, a text, a quick note left at the door says I am here and I still think about you. So what can you do to be a friend? You can be patient and every once and a while reach out to say "I'm here."

Happy -Torture

I found some words to describe how I feel when I receive a memory of my son. I think I feel happy, but its torture at the same time. Happy because I want every bit of anything connected to my son. Tortured because the memories are all I will ever have of Quinn. I won't have any new memories to treasure. Some of the happy tortures I received from friends were photographs of my son, special memories of Quinn they wrote down and sent in a card, ornaments and angles, handmade pictures from his friends and classmates, and photo albums of his life. One special gift was sent to us from a family friend at Christmas time. Opening the box to see a Spiderman ornament, and reading the memory she wrote of Quinn admiring it on her tree, I found as definitely a good example of happy torture. We treasure it and are thankful to her for sharing her sweet memory of our son. I will always have these wonderful memories to look at, because people were thoughtful enough to share. I would rather have the memory and feel the torture of knowing I don't have my son any more than to not have a memory that reminds me how amazing Quinn was every day.

Mother's day was a day I looked forward to receiving homemade gifts from my sons. Quinn's second grade teacher delivered me some happy torture on my first Mother's day without him. It is something special I believe Quinn really wanted me to have. She found the gift he made for me in class for Mother's day at the end of the second grade school year. Somehow it was misplaced and it never made it home to me. It was amazing that she found it the following year just in time for Mother's day.

Quinn's creativity can be seen in some interesting places in our home. The piece of fishing line he used to hang a giant fuzzy, purple spider during Halloween from the light above our kitchen table will always be there. His dirty little hand print will remain on the bottom of the upstairs hallway wall protected by a frame-just where he left it.

Journal Entry–

I put more of your art work in a book today. I remember when you brought work home–even if it was pre-school. I love all of it. I have my Mother's day art, and I want to be as happy as the day you gave it to me. I cry and cry. I wanted to bring these out in another twenty years to show your children what an amazing boy you were. Now I will never have that chance.

I will always treasure all the handmade gifts Quinn created. They hang on the walls, sit on our counters and end tables, and remind me how much I loved receiving each and every one. I look forward to the day when I can look at Quinn's pictures, Lego creations, and drawings and feel happier and less torture.

CHAPTER 3

Year Two

Quinn showing his Legos

Year Two

I don't know how I made it this far. I don't know how I am still living after being without my son for over a year. I don't like to know what day it is, or how many months have passed. I guess if I don't think about it, I can pretend that time just passes. But I don't want to know how much time has passed.

Do I have good days? Some are good, but not all parts of them. A day is good when my surviving son is happy. It's a good day when he doesn't see me looking sad and say, "Do you need a hug mom?" When you lose a child, you have to make the choice to live for your surviving loved ones. Some days I want to make the wrong choice and make this entire nightmare go away; but I think of what it would do to the ones left behind. It isn't my surviving loved one's fault this terrible accident happened, but pain and grief can weigh heavy on choices we have to make. I guess this is what people mean when they tell me I am strong. If this is what being strong is, then I know it would be easy to just be weak.

Journal Entry –

Will and I always talk before he falls asleep. He told me that he sent lots of kisses to my heart. I told him I always need them, and that they help fix the crack in my heart. Will said, "I couldn't be here without you and dad." I told Will that we wouldn't be able to live without him. Then he said, "Maybe next January you won't miss Quinn so much, I am not saying it to be mean, but you just might feel better." I told him that maybe next year we wouldn't be so sad. He said, "Next year maybe you will only have a crack at the top of your heart."

Other grieving parents have told me that they have highs and lows. In this second year I have had more lows than highs. I can go along and be busy with something, but when it's finished and I have nothing to keep my mind occupied, a low will start. I sometimes feel like this means that I have to keep myself busy for the rest of my life just to feel okay. I am on a rollercoaster that forces me to do things, so I climb that steep hill to the top just to free- fall back down to the bottom. Wow, you must be thinking how depressing my life is. It sometimes is, but remember what was ripped away from my normal life. I have to find a new normal, and it isn't filled with relaxing vacations and a big happy family anymore. At least for now.

School started in August, and the first full year of living without Quinn has just passed. Shopping for school related items wasn't much easier this time. It was another school year of Will experiencing what Quinn experienced, which means coming home with the same assignments and projects that Quinn had. I am a bit of a hoarder when it comes to my boys projects, and I recognized almost everything Will was now doing in first grade Quinn did.

October arrived, and it was time to plan a party for Will's seventh birthday. It was important for me to have the party somewhere new. Having another party at the same place would have been uncomfortable and sad for me. Quinn would always be missing from our lives, making the day harder to celebrate.

Some of the people attending Will's party knew our family, and others were unaware of our tragedy. I tried to prepare myself; I knew the questions that would arise from these new people. "How many children do you have?" or "Is Will your only child?" It would have been so easy to say that I have two boys. Saying that would be true, but explaining why Will's brother wasn't at the party was the difficult part. Trying my best to make the day all about Will and pushing my grief aside was difficult. Should I lie about having two children? I couldn't, but the challenge came when I had to answer the question.

I never knew how people would react when I told them that Will has an older brother, but he was killed in a car accident. Some gasp for air. Some said, "I'm sorry," and some didn't know what to say, but felt so uncomfortable that they couldn't get away fast enough.

As hard as it is for some to hear about it, telling people has never been easy for me. I understand that hearing this is shocking, and catches people off guard, but I wish people would just tell me that they can't imagine how I feel, give me a hug, and do their best to focus on the day.

The last part of my second year without Quinn was filled with attempting to try new things. Our friends who are also grieving parents invited us over on Thanksgiving Day. There were no place settings at a fancy dinner table, but paper plates, football and kind people. We were able to get through the day being thankful for having people who understood how we felt, and knew we could get through that day in the nontraditional way.

Eventually I went into my son's classroom to volunteer, I applied for a few jobs and I began to work on Quinn's foundation, Treasures From Quinn. The jobs never went through, but not having to report on a schedule was a good thing at the time. I still had many days where my new life knocked me down, and reporting regularly to a job would not have been the best thing for me.

Volunteering was difficult but, little by little, the kids began to make me feel more comfortable being there. They were so kind, and I could feel that they appreciated me for coming into their classroom. I must say that when my son said, "Mom, why don't you come to my classroom like you used to come in for Quinn's class?", it was the push I needed to try harder. Will gave me that push to keep going and not give up. He reminded me how much he still needed me to be present and a part of his life.

CHAPTER 4

Year Three

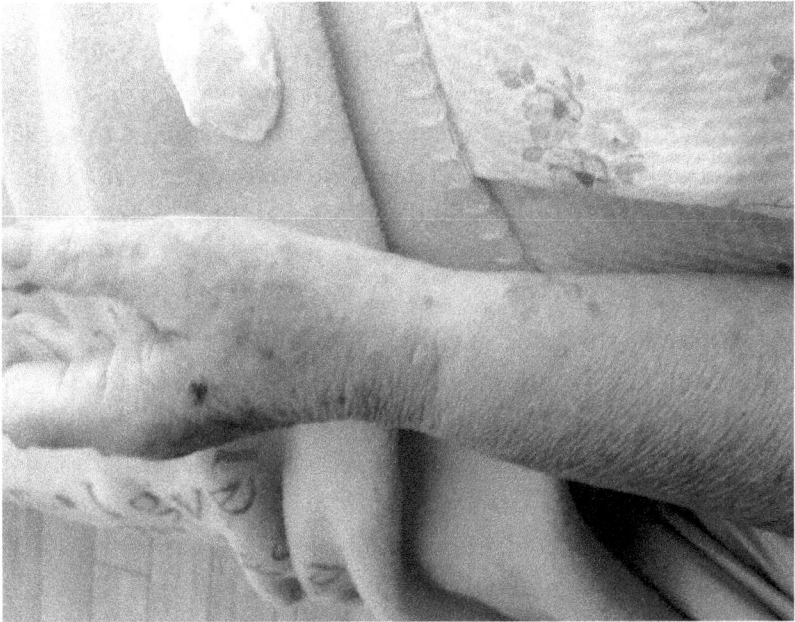

My mom's arm with medical complication

Starting Year Three

I wish I could say that by year three things were great, and back to normal. I can't, and normal isn't a word I used to describe our family. I don't want to say there was no hope, and that we were destined to have a life filled with misery, but life wasn't better for us, it was just different.

Will entered the second grade, and just as we wanted, he would have the same teacher as Quinn. Walking into her classroom for the first time and seeing the empty desk where Quinn sat was too much for me. I quickly excused myself, stepped outside and tried to regain my composure. April had been a good teacher for Quinn. She was aware of his needs and kept in contact with us. Together we worked to manage his assignments in order for him to be successful. We were so grateful that she understood Quinn's needs, and only wanted what was best for him.

Knowing her, we were sure Will would love being in her class as much as Quinn. It wasn't easy to be a part of Will's class that year, but I needed to do my part for him. There were moments of joy, watching how happy Will was when I was involved in an activity in his classroom. The sadness did come, though, when the activity ended, and I was reminded of who I was missing. There would be many ups and downs; I just had to figure out how to keep pushing through to experience more of the ups.

We are learning to live our new normal life. Holiday's, anniversaries and milestones still come, and they can still make it feel like the world is against us. There is no right way to do things. I wanted to escape with my husband and son to a place where nobody knew us. If we didn't want to have Thanksgiving dinner, then we didn't. This may be hard for people to understand, especially if this is a yearly tradition. Being away from my old, normal routine was better for me. I could focus on Will and go about my day without having to celebrate the day or holiday, which didn't feel worthy of celebrating anymore.

Christmas was a holiday we felt we still needed to recognize. Will was still young, and for our family, Christmas was a very important holiday. We recognized the day, but did so in a way that would still provide Will with the joy and excitement it should bring to children. After minimizing the decorations and activities during the first two years, we realized how much joy we were taking away, and how important it was for Will to have these memories. We opened Christmas presents with less tears and began to see how important it was to bring happiness to the day for Will.

As much as I wanted to be the fun mom again who went overboard making cookies, overloading circuits with way too many lights and making special homemade gifts with my children, I just didn't have it in me to go all out. However, I did take note of how and what Will wanted to experience. So together we began to make new traditions. Some baking was done, a few more lights put up, and different homemade gifts were made. These special days can never be what they once were, but I was seeing more clearly how important it was to keep trying to make them special in a new way.

When I talk with other parents who have lost a child, I get mixed answers about how and where they are in this hellish thing we call a grief journey. I remember talking with a dad who lost his daughter (to a drunk driver) toward the end of our first year without Quinn. It was year three of his loss, and he told us that although the first two years were rough, he was beginning to feel less of the heavy grief that consumed him during the first two years. To this day we continue to have a wonderful friendship with this family, and where they have been there for us, we now lean on each other when the grief becomes too devastating for us.

Outpatient Surgery

Just when things didn't seem like they could get even worse, they did. On February 11th 2013 my mom went into the hospital for an outpatient hernia repair. After continuing to recover from the injuries received in the accident, she had a painful hernia that needed to be removed. The morning of the surgery I arrived at the hospital to relieve my sister so she could leave for work.

The surgery was taking longer than expected, but after a while we were told she would be spending the night. The surgeon explained she had a lot of scar tissue, and it took longer to get to the hernia. He also explained he had nicked her bowel, but assured us that he repaired it and she would be fine. He would keep her overnight to recover.

That one night turned into five days of progressive hell. When I finally saw my mom after the surgery, she was pretty heavily medicated. For the next few days, my sister and I took turns being with my mom, asking questions and watching her condition get worse. We were told by the surgeon she needed to get up and walk. She needed to get the anesthesia out of her system. She was in continuous pain and had terrible nausea. We questioned her pain level, why she was nauseous, and why was she still there when the procedure was supposed to be an outpatient surgery. Eventually, from constant vomiting, my mom received a NG tube in her nose, and knowing what I saw coming from the tube, I was concerned.

Less than ten years prior, I had developed a twisted intestine. I was teaching art at the time and remember feeling a lot of pain and nausea. I left school and went directly to my doctor. After seeing my obstetrician, I was given medication for what he assumed was a hematoma and was sent home. I returned to the ER later that evening and was admitted while doctors attempted to find the cause. I lay in the hospital pregnant with Will day after day as numerous doctors attempted to figure out why I was nauseous, vomiting nonstop, in pain and getting worse by the hour. I had the same tube expelling the same nasty substance, and I knew this was something serious. In my case, the doctors figured out what was causing my symptoms, took me into surgery and successfully repaired my intestines, allowing me to recover before too much damage was done.

As for my mom, we wanted answers; we asked why had she not been given further tests to see what was going on. Again we were told-that she just needed to get up and walk. On the fourth day, one of the nurses brought some equipment in hopes that the doctor would order a test that would have showed us through her urine that something was wrong. That test never happened even after constant inquiries to the nurse about when the doctor would be in.

Friday morning came and still no CT scan, no further tests, and she was continuing to get worse. I came in to find my nephew and sister there. I didn't want my nephew to witness his grandmother in that condition any longer, so I said I would stay and sent them home. I approached the nurses, asking for the latest updates, and telling them that something was wrong, because she would get up if she could. Why were no tests performed?

When the nurse making rounds could not get a reading for her blood pressure, I was told that she would come back and try again later. All the signs were there, and now my mom was mumbling and not making sense. I rushed to the nurse's station and said, "Someone needs to get her blood pressure now. Something has to be wrong!" Within a minute of the nurse arriving, I was ushered out of the room, and team of medical staff came rushing in, and she was taken away to intensive care.

Sepsis? How was this possible? I had not been familiar with the signs of sepsis, but she had all but one. Just because she wasn't running a high temperature should not have excluded the medical staff from recognizing the other symptoms. Day after day we called doctors, talked to the nurses about each hour of her day, tried to communicate with my mom, and asked repeatedly, "Why don't they do a CT scan?"

Later that night, we were told to call family, because she probably wouldn't make it through the night. They suspected that the nick in her bowel was leaking and causing the sepsis. They were giving her every medication available to bring her blood pressure to a safe level. They could not move her to do a CT scan to confirm their suspicions. Her organs were failing, and we were told "We're doing everything we can, but your mother is a very sick woman."

Watching her lay there hooked up to the maximum number of infusions and hoping that the numbers would continue to improve, I felt like it was a waste of time. She needed a CT scan, and moving her at that moment could kill her. She survived the horrible accident that almost took her life. She was only given a thirty percent chance of survival then, and now her chances were less.

Somehow she made it through the night, and after a long day of waiting, they made the decision that if she was going to have a chance to survive, she needed the CT scan to find the exact cause of her condition. I watched as they rolled her down the long hallway with a team of doctors surrounding her bed trying to keep her alive on the way to the scan. Waiting was painful. She made it through the scan, but we were told that she may not make it through the night. The scan showed surgery, even though life threatening, was necessary to save her life. The surgeon never admitted the repair to her bowel he nicked was the cause of the leak. Supposedly, it was another leak right near that area. In my opinion, it was too much of a coincidence to be "another leak." So once again we were told to say our good byes as she may not survive the surgery.

Many times over the next few months I would question myself about something I said to my mother before they wheeled her off to surgery to try and repair her bowel. I didn't know how much she could comprehend, but I leaned over her and told her, "I already lost my son and I don't have a father anymore, and I need a mother."

For as much as she doesn't remember about what she went through over that year, she told me later that she did hear me, and so she fought. What I said that night, I questioned many times over the next year. To witness the pain, tests, complications and surgeries she encountered from the moment I asked her to fight was something I never would have asked if I could have predicted the hell she encountered that year.

That year took so much from all of us. It was a strain on our marriages, our children, and our mental wellbeing. So many hours away from home, taking on financial and daily responsibilities for my mother along with having to make all medical decisions on her behalf was draining and mentally damaging.

What I found most disturbing was to witness how the level of care my mother received seemed to be affected by our presence. Day after day we sat by her bedside, rotating shifts with her brothers and sisters who flew in to be by her side. We educated ourselves by asking questions, inquiring with other doctors and researching her condition. I can recall many times when I would walk into my mother's ICU room and she would be in distress, alarms going off with no nurse in the room, or outside in the hall. One of the scariest times was when her ventilator alarm was sounding because the tube attached to her throat had popped off. This was her breathing support as she wasn't breathing on her own. As I ran to the door and looked up and down the hall, I saw no medical staff in sight. I called for help, but no one responded. I ran back to my mom's bedside, picked up the tube and attempted to reconnect it. Although the alarm continued to sound, I thought it was reattached, so I ran to the hall again calling a nurse out of the closest room. After all that my mom was doing to try to stay alive, I wondered how could this happen?

The need to spend so much time at the hospital making sure she was getting the care she needed was exhausting. We began to keep a log of her stats, medications, how often she was turned in bed, how often her wounds were cleaned, and more. She was in ICU, and still mistakes were made. So many little things that could have turned into major infections such as the elastic band holding on her ventilation tube that was cutting into her ear went unnoticed until I brought it to the nurse's attention.

Decisions had to be made, and one major decision included

firing her nephrology team. It would be the most important decision that I believed saved her life and set her in the right direction for a chance at recovery. Thanks to good friends with helpful advice and connections, we were able to hire a new nephrology team to treat my mom. Within a few days she showed signs of improvement. Her organs that failed began to show signs of recovery.

From here on in, it wasn't all good news, but at least it wasn't an uphill battle. Watching my mom lay in a bed, machines breathing for her, infusions feeding her, filling with so much fluid that it oozed out of her skin, I found myself depressed and infuriated. Everyone who saw her witnessed her horrific appearance and this continued to distort the person we all knew. These are the memories my mom does not recall, but they are more images that can never be erased from my mind. Not being able to speak, eat or take a sip of water, not even being able to write because her hands were swollen like balloons made communicating with my mom difficult.

We never gave up, and I couldn't understand why she didn't. She struggled to get us to understand her. We used a white board to show her pictures in hopes that she would respond when we pointed to an area that might be causing her pain. We stayed on top of what felt like everything, and somehow she had improved enough to be moved. Because she was still on a ventilator, she was moved to another ICU room in a different hospital where she would have the best chance to be weaned off of the ventilator.

From the moment we arrived, mistakes were made. Her room was not set up and ready to accommodate her needs. The staff seemed annoyed as it was almost shift change, and people had to be rounded up to set up the equipment for her ventilator and infusions. Even the EMTs from the ambulance transport were annoyed that her ventilator wasn't set up as she was only on a limited pump intended for the ambulance ride over. Her IV source of nourishment was not available, her medical records and history were nowhere to be found, and even thought she was in a specialized hospital known for treating patients in her condition, they did not have my trust. I did my research on this place, visited many times, and felt confident that my mom would receive the care and treatment she needed to continue to improve. They failed miserably from the minute we arrived, and I knew our days of taking shifts by her bedside were not over.

Over the next few months our family rotated in and out of the hospital almost around the clock, keeping notes on what medication she was given, or was not given. It was a struggle to get the services she needed. We gave constant reminders that she did not receive her physical therapy, even though it was part of her treatment plan. I felt like if we didn't ask for something as simple as changing her bed sheets, then it would not be done.

I did things for my mom that otherwise were ignored. I learned my way around the ICU, fetched towels, sheets, gloves, cups, ice and more. Of course, I was always willing to help, but coming in day after day to hear about a list of things the nurses and staff neglected to do was unacceptable.

I felt the need to learn how to reposition my mom in bed so she wouldn't get bed sores. I learned how to check her wounds as they were healing for signs of infection. I was not an employee of the hospital, not paid for my services, and did not enjoy doing the jobs hospital staff should have been doing. What bothered me most was the fact that instead of visiting with my mom it was necessary for me to do a check list every time I came in to see her, making sure her needs were attended to. Over her stay in that particular hospital, I watched many patients pass away. Because I was there so often it, saddened me to see patience's in the ICU lying alone without visitors and family by their side. I can only imagine the list of things the staff neglected to do for these people. Each day when I came in to see another empty bed, it was another reminder of why our family needed to be there to be my mom's voice.

CHAPTER 5

Year Four

Sunset over the cruise ship rail

A Tough Year

Year four started and ended rough. A new year, another year without. There will always be a holiday, birthday, anniversary, or school event that just happens. To say these days stir up memories and sadness is putting it lightly. Sure, I remembered all the wonderful things we all did as a family, and in my mind I smile, but on the outside I am only human and I can't hide the disappointment and sadness of what I wish I could have on these days. Life will happen, and maybe this was just a year where I felt the world was against me.

I started 2014 without my first and best canine buddy, Chili Pepper. Chili passed away in December. He would have turned 14 years old on January 5th. Chili was a gift from my parents back in 2000. As a child, I grew up with our family dogs, and Chili came into my life when I really needed him. Chili gave me love when he knew I was down. At that time, I was struggling with the fact that everyone around me was getting pregnant or having a baby, and it just wasn't happening for me.

People would say that he was my first baby. He was, but of the canine type, because Quinn was born the following November. Chili enjoyed life with our family for almost 14 years. Chili loved Quinn, and watched over him day and night, even squeezing in next to us as I fed Quinn in the rocking chair. It was also hard to lose Chili, because he was a part of Quinn's entire short life. But saying goodbye to Chili is only temporary. I believe that he is now with Quinn, and we will all be together again someday.

After accepting that I was needed here, I decided to join our country club gym. Some of the classes they offered like body combat and body attack sounded like just what I needed to work out my anger. From the very first class, I knew this was where I could go to fight out my stress and anger. Every punch and kick had a face and a name to it.

If people could hear who I was yelling at in my head I am sure I would have been asked to leave. I wish so many times I could have yelled out the names of all the people involved at General Motors who I believed contributed to my son and father's death. I found myself fighting for my son in a physical way that wasn't illegal. That one hour of each day I exhausted myself fighting through all my anger, and it was a lot! I looked forward to every class as they had become therapeutic in releasing my frustrations and so I didn't bring all the anger home. Despite my efforts to work out my anger at the gym, the depression and anger stayed with me, so I continued therapy, combat classes and volunteering with the dogs, hoping things would get better.

The school year ended for Will in late May. My main focus was on finding activities to keep him busy, and planning a vacation where we wouldn't have to drive a long distance to get there. My other focus was waiting to go to trial with General Motors, which was scheduled for early July.

I was as prepared as I could be to go to trial and say what I needed to say, but a phone call we received from our lawyers ended with the decision not to go to trial. I did have a say in the decision, but most of my family had made up their minds, and there would be no trial.

In the beginning of July, once again, I was knocked down and saddened with the loss of my good friend and neighbor, Tina. Tina fought breast cancer with all she had. Tina was watching our pups while we were away that July in 2010, and I had sent her a text telling her that we would be home soon. The accident happened less than a half hour after my text. I had no idea of the battle Tina was just beginning to go through when she got the phone call. Tina had already been diagnosed with cancer, but didn't tell me until a few years later. She said with all that we had been through, she didn't want anything else to upset me. Something I can't ignore is the day Tina's husband, Keith, called to tell me she had gotten worse and she wasn't going to make it. I hung up the phone, told my husband the sad news, and said I think I know what day she will pass. Tina passed just after midnight, and the date was July 3rd, the same date Quinn passed. I believe Quinn was there to help her cross over, and that they are taking care of each other. She gave so much of herself, and I miss her every day.

Quinn with Chili Pepper

I wondered why me? and how much more punishment was I supposed to be able to take. I wanted to escape to a place where nobody knew us. A place where no one would know our family's tragedy, and no one would know the hell I was running from. I booked a trip, and we left for Hawaii. I wanted to find some sort of peace and anything to lessen the sadness.

Hawaii is a beautiful place, and it's a shame that all the heaviness, anger and grief made it difficult to appreciate. Of course, one of my main priorities was seeing that Will was busy and having fun. The times when Will was excited and enjoying this beautiful place were times anger and sadness eased.

Summer ended and school was back in session for Will. Many emotions I had never felt before in my life began to rise to the surface. A heaviness came rushing back beginning late October, and it lasted for the rest of the year. I can only describe it as depression mixed with anger and a touch of insanity. It was as if I were weighed down by fifty pound weights, so full of anger, rage and sadness that I didn't know whether to punch the wall or cry myself to sleep. I needed to find an outlet, because I didn't want the solution to be checking myself in to an asylum.

My birthday and Will's birthday had just passed in October and now it would only get harder the rest of the year. November was Quinn's birthday and Thanksgiving. In December was Christmas. November was hard enough to get through, and then the cheery holidays were near. I didn't want to decorate; I wanted to smash the Christmas lights, not hang them. I wanted to sleep and not wake up until it was all over.

But what was I thinking? I had Will, who had just turned ten and loved Christmas. I didn't know how I was going to find the strength to give him the Christmas he deserved. Christmas came and went with some lights outside and a live tree inside. The tree did have lights, but only five ornaments were hung. I had no holiday spirit and no energy or desire to hang more ornaments. I thought it would get easier each year, but I now knew better. I could only do the best I could, and hope that next year would be easier.

The Phone Call

The time came for a decision. Our remaining family members were all on the conference call. There was no celebrating for me. I listened to our lawyers talk about how it came down to the last minute, and here is what GM is offering. I remember being asked, "How does everyone feel?"

I spoke up and said, "I am not happy." I remember others mumbling and saying okay. Then there was silence. It was difficult to speak, but I whimpered out, "I don't want to settle, I want to go to trial."

I can't imagine anyone being totally shocked because, I made it clear that going to trial was what I wanted. I didn't want to be another lawsuit settlement checked off General Motors list. Why should they win?

I was told, "They don't win, because they would have to pay." Pay for what the lives of my father and young son who never got to live past eight years old? I listened to my family members and lawyers try to convince me that this was the best thing to do.

"Even if we win, they will appeal," they said. "This could go on for another five years. We don't want you to have to go through this again."

Again? I have never stopped going through this! This will never end for me, and there is no moving forward. Some of my family members stated that they just wanted to put this in the past and move forward, but there is no moving past this for me. I continue to live with all the misery this tragedy brought me every day of my life.

I cried, cursed, pleaded and screamed on the phone, hoping my family and lawyers would support me and change their minds about settling with GM-not letting them win. I needed my say in court, but that day never happened. The mental and physical pain that I felt during the hour long conference call urging, petitioning, and pleading with my family and lawyers to convince them of the reasons why I needed to go to court almost depleted me. I have never felt such helplessness and rage at the same time. The last thing I said on the phone was, "I can't win."

I decided I needed time away from everyone. I only had enough strength to breathe for my husband and son. I was no longer the one who worried about putting others first as I always did. I did not speak or see the rest of my family for over a month. It was hard to deal with everyday life without taking out my rage on the people I loved.

After packing my family- the three of us now- and leaving the state for ten days I returned home feeling the same anger and disappointment I felt before we left. How was I ever supposed to try to move forward? There was never getting past it, and I sure saw no outlet for how to go on knowing I would never get my say.

Some people may say, "This too shall pass, or " Time heals everything," I say no and no! I was told that my family didn't want me to have to relive it all over again, the Arizona court system is really tough, and they may try to paint me as a bad mother. My family said, "They will try to say it was your fault. The jury might not be able to rule in your favor. GM will try to give them reasonable doubt."

I already had my opinions about the GM lawyers. GM was no longer the company my dad worked so hard for most of his life; I saw it as my enemy. They had no interest in taking responsibility for my father or son's deaths-so much for taking care of a loyal GM employee.

Whatever they had to say, I was ready to fight. I didn't think it would be sugar coated to shield my feelings. Did I want more stress and sadness? No, but I had a story to tell. I did nothing wrong, and my dad and son didn't deserve to die. The time had come to expose General Motors for what I believed they did wrong. I had been told about enough cases where innocent people were asked questions that make them seem at fault.

What were my faults? My faults were going on a family vacation, riding in what we were told to be a safe vehicle. Every one of us were seat belted in while riding the speed limit. No laws were broken, no distracted driver, intoxicated driver, no driving offences. Yes, we all had clean records, so they could have done their best to say otherwise, but we were the victims here, not General Motors.

What the hell did I have to lose? I wanted to tell my side. I wanted the chance to tell about the hell we experienced starting on that 3rd day in July. I wanted to tell how a family trip that was so memorable ended with the reoccurring nightmare we live every day. My dad was a person, not someone who had a price tag. My son was a little boy who had so much living to do. Money could not replace him.

I have spent years in therapy trying to deal with what I do remember, and I remember it all. From the loud noise to the first slam followed by several rolls. I relive it every day when I look at the scars on any one of our bodies. I see it in my face that looks as if it has aged twenty years, even though it's only been a few. The loss of my child is the most painful thing- both physically and mentally-that I have ever experienced.

To see my son alive as he was airlifted to the hospital and not to be told anything until the next morning was mentally painful. Forget the physical injuries I had suffered. I wanted to know how my family members were. I had so much anxiety about needing to know how my family was that I didn't feel a lot of pain at the time. I remember calling out to any nurse who would walk by in the hallway to please find out how my son was. They knew my son had passed, but no one would tell me anything. So no, this will not pass, and I will have to learn to deal with not getting my say in court, and I will never be happy about that.

The Trial that Didn't Happen

The third day of July 2014 was approaching, and I was ready to have my say in court. Ready to tell the court and General Motors who I was, who we were, and all about my son and father who I believed they killed. Many stressful years had passed, many depositions, meetings, phone calls, and questions answered over and over again. I was so ready.

Then the day before our trial was to begin the phone call came. I was just finishing a session with my therapist when my cell phone rang. When I answered it, my husband said, "Our lawyers called, the other party wants to settle, come home and we will have a conference call in one hour."

My heart dropped and I immediately wanted to throw up. As I drove home, I felt overwhelming anger as my mind raced. Why the hell did they wait until the day before trial to offer a settlement? I said from the beginning I never wanted to settle, because it wasn't about the money. This was about the deaths of my dad and eight-year-old son. Deaths which I believe could have been prevented.

General Motors website states, "Our story starts on November 18, 2010, when we completed the world's largest public offering, emerging with a solid financial foundation that enables us to produce great vehicles for our customers and building a bright future for our employees, partners and shareholders. Leading the way is our seasoned leadership team who set high standards for our company so that we can give you the best cars and trucks. This means that we are committed to delivering vehicles with compelling designs, flawless quality and reliability, and leading in safety, fuel economy and infotainment features."

Their story started four months and fifteen days too late for my father and son. They say they are "committed to delivering vehicles with flawless quality, and leading in safety." GM's website also reads, "GM's Commitment to Safety- Quality and safety are at the top of the agenda at GM. We put customers at the center of everything we do. We listen intently to our customers' needs. Each interaction matters. Safety and quality are foundational commitments, never compromised." If "safety is at the top of their agenda, and safety is never compromised," then I question why they don't make their tire aging policy retroactive? Five years before in 2005, the standard was to adopt a six year tire aging policy, and GM refused to join. How can they stand by their statement, "Customer safety is our number one priority"?

After arriving at home, I told my husband that not only was I disgusted, but really angry. I called my sister and told her that I did not want to settle. I didn't think this would be a surprise to anyone. After years of suffering through questions and accusations about everything from my childhood, personal life, family history and more, I wasn't willing to settle.

It would be like quitting. I couldn't fathom how settling after all these years would even be a question. What amount of money would bring back my son and father? I explained to my sister that I wasn't happy and was prepared for court. I didn't want to settle.

She asked me if my mom knew about this. I told her, "How could she not." She informed me of my mom's reaction to the news. When she told me that mom was actually praying that GM would settle, I was confused and angry. She actually placed a statue next to the phone, praying that it would happen.

When I called my mom, she asked me how I felt. I don't know how to describe the rage I was feeling. I said, "I am not happy. I don't want to settle!" Sure, I figured my mom didn't want to go through trial and have terrible memories come up; no one would, but I figured she would do it for me.

I understood my mother's health issues, and knew that if this trial was too stressful and caused her heath to worsen, she could be excused medically from having to attend court. I was willing to speak for the entire family. This was something I needed to do. We were all in this together, but after all was said and done; I realized I was pretty much alone. The reasonable side of me thought, they just don't get it. How can any amount of money be enough for the loss of my dad and son? As I said before, it was never about the money.

It took many years for me to get to where I am today. So many times I wanted to give up and end my life. What I chose to do was fight. The law suit against GM was my fight. Every time I saw on the news or read about another recall from GM it made me want to fight more. I thought if I could show GM that I wasn't going away, that this trial would happen, and the public would be informed. I had nothing to hide. By getting the word out, this could be a chance to save other families from experiencing an accident like ours.

I had so much to tell, but what I had to say, they wouldn't want to hear. I cannot forget what I experienced, saw and felt. I cannot forget what it felt like to hear my father's last words and feel the vehicle slam and roll over and over again. I cannot erase the screams and moans of my family from my memory. I can't erase what I saw after the roof crushed my father, and how the broken glass left Will bleeding. I can't erase the image of my family trapped inside the truck. As the paramedics took Quinn to the helicopter, I never thought that would be the last time I would see my son.

This was the last day of our family trip. We were all buckled in after our last stop to fuel up to get home. We were less than two hours from home, and we were excited to see our puppies and tell everyone about the great week we all had. What the hell happened? We did nothing wrong. We were a happy family on our way back from vacation. We were supposed to be in a safe vehicle.

An article titled "Another Domino Falls: GM Adds Tire Age Warning" was published by Sean Kane because of our horrific crash. In part it said, "GM began warning its customers about the dangers of tire aging overseas in the early 1990s. They stated that a spare wheel which has not been used for six years should be used only in emergencies and to drive slowly when using such tires. Recently, GM became the last of the American automakers to add a tire age warning to the owner's manuals of its 2013 U.S. models. A retired GM tire and wheel engineer, who consults as a corporate representative, says he knows of no current plan to promote or make known the recommendation beyond the pages of the 2013 owner's manuals. There will be no public statement as there was five years ago to explain why it wasn't adopting a tire age recommendation. This would leave the majority of its customers uninformed".

Exactly, uninformed! The article continues, "Even members of the GM community – such as John Taylor and his family – would be left vulnerable to an entirely preventable crash." The words from the article, "entirely preventable crash" will haunt me forever.

And finally the article said "So, in 2005 when the industry standard was to adopt a 6-year tire aging policy for the safety of consumers and GM refuses to join and, more particularly, refuses to conduct any testing or research to determine the appropriate aging standard in the intervening 7 years, what do you call GM?" I know I have many names for them. "When GM finally adopts a 6-year tire aging policy, it has no intention of any retroactive application of the policy to protect owners of older GM vehicles." These statements once again remind me that the safety of the American public is not GM's priority.

Getting My Say

This book was a way for me to get my say. I never planned to write a book about grief, the dangers of an unsafe vehicle company, and why I believe I am still here today. If my story is read and one person tells another person, then little by little I will get my say. If I can help someone else feel they are not alone after losing a child, family member or loved one, I am getting my say. If one person reads my story and thinks twice, does more research, checks safety records when thinking about buying a GM vehicle, then I got my say. I am happy to announce that our family will never buy or drive another GM vehicle.

Even though I never did get my say in court, I think some of my words in this book tell our story. It's the story of how our close family of six was reduced to a sad family of four. No more father for me, father-in-law for Bill, husband for my mom, grandfather for Will, son for my husband and myself, brother for Will and grandson for my mother. Relationships strained by grief destroyed the family we once were. A family destroyed in one afternoon that was supposed to be the end to a vacation filled with a lifetime of memories.

I do have some amazing memories of playing and digging for treasures on the beach with my family, watching my dad teaching Quinn to fish, riding our bikes up and down the beach, and eating our favorite sea food at dinner. Thinking of these memories used to make me sob. Now I can recall these memories and cry less with some happier tears. I know that my dad and Quinn want me to try and continue to live with less anger and sadness. I do things for the people I love every day of my life. I think I will be trying to do this for the rest of my life.

My Statement

Because I never got my say in court I am writing what I would have expressed if I had the chance. I am sure this would have been beyond difficult for me to say, but I believe through a lot of anger and tears I would have been able to say what needed to be said.

- My name is Susanne Levi, and my husband is Bill.
- I am a mom, and my children are my full time job. My son's names are Quinn and Will.
- My mom is Eileen, my dad is John.
- I have never been arrested, never in trouble with the law. I follow the rules.
- My husband and I bought what we thought was a safe family vehicle. We bought a Chevy Trailblazer from General Motors, the company my father worked for 38 years. My dad was a proud GM employee, and insisted on buying American and supporting GM, the company he was loyal to.
- On July 3rd 2010, my family had a rollover accident in our Chevy Trailblazer on our way home from vacation.
- My eight-year-old son, Quinn, and father were killed. I died that day, and I can never be who I once was.
- I will never forget that devastating day, and will never be able to put this passed me. I miss my son every minute of the day. I miss hearing his voice, seeing his smile and watching him grow.
- I miss going to my parents' house where Quinn was always happy to see something new his Pappy had to show him. They had a great relationship. I miss that very much.
- I can remember going with my family to the General Motors building in Trenton New Jersey at a young age. We went there to learn about vehicle safety and the importance of wearing

seatbelts. From that day on, our family never went without our seatbelts. Back then General Motors was a company our family was proud to support. They seemed to have the safety of the American public as a priority.

• I do not believe General Motors put the safety of the public, and definitely not the safety of my family first with the choices they made when they built our family's Chevy Trailblazer.

• Problems can arise during the building process, but when problems are brought to the company's attention, they should not be ignored.

• The lives of my son, Quinn, and father, John, were not worth NOTHING! They had so much living to do, and I feel General Motors took this away from all of us.

• My son had sensory processing disorder. He worked hard every day to fix the problems he faced. As parents we chose to do something about Quinn's disability. We didn't choose to ignore the problem. He was in brain training, and we began to see him overcome the struggles he faced.

• I will never again have complete family vacations, holidays, or milestones. My son, Will, now must grow up without his brother. I will never see my eight-year-old son grow up, and I am physically and mentally tormented knowing this.

• I never want to drive, and will never recommend or purchase another General Motors vehicle. I am ashamed of what this company ignored and grieve with other families who have lost loved ones and hope no more lives are taken because of safety choices General Motors decided to ignore.

CHAPTER 6

Year Five

Turtle in Hawaii

Do I have to be busy for the rest of my life?

My friend, Taunya's daughter, Ellie, was killed in a car accident. Ellie was a few short days from her fourth birthday when she was hit by a driver who had been drinking, speeding and driving recklessly. After meeting her at the previous year's event, I now helped with the fund raiser that honored her daughter. This was a way for me to channel my anger by being busy and turning it into something positive. My trust in people had been tainted after our car accident, and I was furious at the people I believe were responsible for my son's death.

I could relate to how Taunya felt, and admired her strength and courage to help others. I often felt the only way to keep going was to keep myself busy. If I was busy helping other people, then my life didn't slow down enough for me to think about my reality. I began to look for ways to help other people who had suffered or were suffering with the loss of a loved one. I threw myself into whatever cause I could help with.

Somehow being around other parents who have suffered a loss was somewhat of a safe place for me to be. I felt understood and not at all judged. I listened and they listened, and we didn't feel so alone. When I hear about parents who have lost their child, I can now reach out and say I am available for them. When I couldn't get out of bed and saw no hope, I was offered the chance to meet with a mom who had lost her child. This mom was Taunya, and I was introduced to her about six months after my son was killed. She was suffering and grieving the loss of her daughter, and understood what I was feeling and wanted to help. I will never forget her words when I met her at the charity tea held in her daughters honor. I stood in line as she was thanking people for attending, and my neighbor introduced me. All she said was, "I am not even going to ask you how you are." She then gave me a big hug and offered to take my number to meet sometime. She is now one of my dearest friends.

One of my biggest fears is that Quinn will be forgotten. I believed if I pushed myself to help others, it was a way of honoring Quinn and, as I've said I would keep busy so that I wouldn't think about how empty my life was without him. At the same time I, had a better understanding for other people's grief, whether it was for the loss of a loved one, or battling a disease.

My therapist cautioned me about being too busy. I didn't understand what was so wrong about being busy. If I was busy,

I wouldn't have time to crawl back into my black hole where I was shut off from the world of harmful people. When I stayed busy, I pushed myself to do more things, because it was a way of remembering and bringing awareness about the people who were taken from us.

I have always been an animal lover, and after adopting our third dog, I learned about a rescue named HALO. Halo stands for Helping Animals Live On. For me, HALO was a place I could go where I was needed and loved by all. No one judged me or yelled at me, and I could talk about whatever I needed to with all my four legged friends who were always happy to see me. Volunteering for HALO was something new to keep me busy, but it was a good type of busy for me.

Helping to care for the animals that craved human interaction was some of the best therapy I have gotten. These poor animals, most of whom have been left on the streets or abused, get a second chance at life with HALO. This was a way for me to help, and in return, I felt like I was needed and could make a difference.

PART TWO

ADVICE

CHAPTER 7

Holidays

Our family at the Polar Express

Holidays

Quinn and Will on Christmas morning

Nothing will ever be the same for the parents who have lost a child. Holidays were special days we all spent as a family. Don't expect the grieving family to want to participate in the routine family holiday traditions. And please don't expect the family to be happy for you.

Imagine sitting down to Thanksgiving dinner when everyone tells what they are thankful for and are surrounded by their loved ones. The year before my son passed his birthday fell on Thanksgiving day. It was a very special and memorable day for us, but it's a day we will never be able to celebrate again. Please don't feel that the grieving family is ruining your holiday. For us it felt like every day was ruined.

Let the parents decide when and if they want to join you. You may extend the offer, but for me I wanted the day to be over as soon as possible. My choice was to escape to somewhere, but not too far away. Our driving long distances to get to a vacation were over. We went to a local resort on many holidays so Will could be busy with activities, and we didn't need to recognize the day. Nobody had to sit down at a fancy table and eat turkey, or tell what they were thankful for. For us, at the time, the focus was on Will, and making it through the day.

Christmas was our family's favorite holiday. Our first Christmas without Quinn was devastating. I had no desire to put out decorations or send cards. Decorating the house inside and out was what we used to do all together. The boys would be so excited when we would put lights outside and it seemed like every year we would add something new. The year after we lost Quinn no boxes were opened, no Christmas card picture was taken, no train set was under the tree.

Each time I noticed another neighbor decorating their house, it was another reminder of what I had lost. You see everyone goes back to their life the way it was. At least for me this is how I saw it at the time. For me my life would never be the same. If you have other children, you have to make a choice of what is best for them. For my husband and, I it meant taking Will to the store and letting him pick out some decorations that he wanted to see put out. How do you say to a six year old that we don't want to have Christmas because your brother isn't here?

We couldn't bear to open last year's decorations and have the memories remind us every day even more of what we had lost, but sometimes you have to do what is best for your surviving child. As much as it hurt to put up a string of lights outside and around our tree, we did it because Will asked, "Why don't we have any lights outside?" As a friend of the family, use your best judgment, but I wouldn't go to the house all full of holiday cheer yelling Merry Christmas! Remember, probably most parents' who have lost a child don't want to be wished a Merry Christmas.

My suggestion is to support the parents by helping their surviving child. Christmas is an exciting time especially for young children. I was thankful for the little special treats friends left at the door for our son. They offered to take Will out to see Christmas lights, and invited him to join their family's fun traditions. They did the special things for him that my husband and I were not able to do. They helped to make Christmas a little less sad for Will.

One special lady named Mary often left surprises at our front door. She too had suffered loss in her life, and knew how leaving special treats and messages at our door would make Will's day. The packages she left at our door had meaning and were reminders to us that Quinn would not be forgotten.

Journal Entry–

Mary came by today. She brought food, cookies and a bag full of Valentine treats for Will. She is another amazing person who has had to deal with losing a loved one. She never forgets us. She does so much for us and Will. I wonder how she can be so giving and thoughtful and be the role model to so many that she is? She had to suffer and so many years later it still comes back to her. I will never understand why good people are punished.

I can speak to Mary without crying the entire time. She does things for Will that I want to, but can't. The sweet little extra special holiday things that I don't want to celebrate. I don't want to celebrate anything. I would just let the days pass if I could.

How do you erase someone from your life? You can't and don't. The first Christmas without Quinn I made small note cards with a picture Quinn had drawn of Santa's sleigh and reindeer printed up. I mailed these out to family and friends with stamped return envelopes. I asked that they write a special memory of Quinn so we could put them in his stocking that hung from our fireplace.

I was saddened, angry and confused when so many did not come back. I guess I never realized how hard it was for people to put a memory of my loving child on a small piece of paper. Many months later, one of his teachers came to me and told me he wanted me to know he hadn't forgotten about the note card, but that it was still sitting on his counter. He couldn't think of the right words to use to describe so many memories Quinn made for him.

It made me feel better knowing he didn't just put it aside, but I still wanted to hear whatever his thoughts were, even if it was just a sentence or two. So don't be afraid to send a note, pictures or any memory of the child to the parents. I treasured anything I received of Quinn's whether it was a picture, a note about something he did, or an old paper one of his teachers found in the file cabinet. Yes I cried, but it was a good cry.

May we always remember Quinn. He loved to give and make each day better for the people he loved.

We Love and miss you Quinn,
The Dominguez Family

We will always remember how excited Quinn was on his birthday with the dollar bill piñata and huge marshmallows. As soon as we walked in the door, he was telling us all about the fun things that he had in store for his party. He was so proud of the dollar piñata and how Susanne put it together for him. We joked about if it was a real dollar bill what would we buy and if any store would take it. Then as night came around, it was time for roasting marshmallows. The marshmallows were huge and Quinn was so excited. He had a blast roasting the marshmallows without catching them on fire. Quinn made sure Heather and Andrew didn't get to close to the fire. He always made us feel like we were family. No matter how much time would pass since we saw each other last. Till this day, Heather and Andrew always mention Quinn's name whenever we roast marshmallows outside on the fire pit. Quinn will live in our hearts and minds forever.

God makes Angels to keep us safe. Quinn is our little Angel ♡

May we always remember Quinn. He loved to give and make each day better for the people he loved. 12/10

Dear Quinn,
There are so many memories I could choose to write about. I still have the leaf you gave me up on my bulletin board. The one memory that really sticks out in my mind is the time you came in the Health Center and were resting on one of the cots. We were talking about legos and what you had been drawing that day when you stopped and said, "Nurse Tracey, do you know what this place needs?" No, Quinn, tell me what this place needs," I replied. You said, "This place needs a TV up there →

(pointing above the upper cabinets), so when kids come in they won't be so bored!" That made me laugh. See Quinn, you always had a way of making people smile or laugh. You have such a big heart.

I can't tell you how many times this school year I would be sitting at my desk and hear the door open, hoping it was you walking in. I miss you terribly buddy.

Love
Nurse Tracey

Note Cards

Our Last Family Christmas picture

CHAPTER 8

Grieving

Dragonfly

Everyone Grieves Differently and in Their Own Time

Everyone grieves differently and in their own time. Don't judge, you can't and don't know what they are feeling. If you see a parent out shopping one day, don't think they are all better. At first when I would go out to grocery shop, I wished I could be invisible. I could not go back to the same store I had shopped at before I lost my son. Most people would not understand why, but everywhere I went I would miss not seeing my son there. Something as simple as the thought of having to walk past the kids' play center, somewhere Quinn would never go again, was too much for me to handle. I started to shop at a new store where I had not been before with my son.

Many times when I saw someone I knew, I would go down a different isle to avoid them. I didn't want to answer the question most everyone asks: How are you? I learned I was going to bump into friends and neighbors, so I eventually learned to say hi without crying. One of the best things anyone who saw me could do or say was not ask me how I was, but maybe give a quick hug or a put a gentle hand on my shoulder, and to be brief and just say they were thinking about our family.

Life after losing a child makes doing routine things difficult. Back to school shopping, birthday parties, class picture day, celebrating holidays, vacation, and even hearing another parent call their child the same name as the child you lost. I remember hearing a dad call out for his son named Quinn in the Lego toy aisle. It took my breath away and made me freeze as I watched for his Quinn to come down the aisle. My first trip to Target to get Will some things for school was distressing. Everywhere I looked I saw clothes, supplies and more things that I would have picked up for Quinn. These are examples of things parents do all the time without ever thinking how they would feel doing them without their child. You might think "that's ridiculous, but imagine how different your day would be. So be patient and try to understand what your life would be like without your child. Don't judge because you have your child, making it impossible to fully understand what a parent continues to go through. There is no good time to move on. No set time to start living life again. Parents will try to start living there new "normal" life when they are ready.

Marriages and Families Feel Stress

After the crash, the moment the truck stopped rolling, worrying about my family was my focus. I had to take charge, assess the situation and get moving. Not having control over what was happening to each of my family members was shattering. Because I was the mom, I needed to be the strong one and do my job to get to everyone and provide the information to fix the situation. Things didn't happen that way.

I wasn't alone, but I felt alone. The rest of my family was trapped inside the vehicle, and I didn't have anyone there to help me fix the problems. I was also alone in the hospital. I was told not to speak to my husband, and could not see my boys, my mom or my dad. I begged, but could not even speak to my sister who had arrived at the hospital. The stress of being alone and not able to do my job was overwhelming.

Eventually, I learned the devastating news that two of my family members passed in the accident, my mom was given a 30% chance to live, and my husband was sedated because he needed surgery. Not only was I stressed, but I was alone.

My next task was to tell my husband that Quinn and my dad were gone. I saw my mom hooked up to machines, unaware of any one's condition. Then it was time to tell Will that his brother had passed. It was one of the most difficult days of my life.

Loss extends to the whole family, and is especially challenging for couples. Husbands and wives may not always grieve the same. There were days, early on, when both my husband and I were both in the same place, and all we could do was sit next to each other in silence, cry on each other's shoulders, and know that we were in this together.

Everyday life can easily get in the way and cause arguments. Neither of us wanted to go out, cook, clean, pay bills or do laundry. Not only were we physically injured, but mentally we had no desire to do the things we had always done. Many days it took all we had to get out of bed, get dressed and take Will to school. We saved all of our energy for Will.

Grudges can develop toward the spouse who sits on the couch deep in grief ignoring everyday tasks that should be done. I would say that being kind and patient is important. My husband and I had each other to grieve with. So if we would have done something such as yell at each other over who was going to take out the trash, it would have only made us angry and feel more alone. We had to accept that some days we wouldn't be on the same page, but it wasn't easy.

I have seen the statistics of how many marriages fall apart after the loss of a child, and I can easily see why it happens. I had to learn that if my husband wanted to sleep all afternoon to escape the day, it was ok. It wasn't my job to tell him how to move forward. I had many of those days myself, and he had to accept that I needed to escape too. There is no instruction manual, and no right way to get through the day. For me, knowing both of us were handed this grief (we never asked for) meant we had to figure out how to survive our marriage, parenting and how to go on together. We learned to respect our differences.

After speaking with other parents who have lost a child, I learned about many ways parents attempt to get relief from their grief. Alcohol, prescription medications, working long hours, finding a new hobby, volunteering, and moving to a new place are just a few examples of how parents try to escape from grief. Some or all of these examples can add stress to a marriage.

There were often times my husband and I were in different stages in our grief. Many times he wanted to have a few beers, check out and fall asleep. I resented him because all of the responsibilities, including taking care of Will, fell on me. I was hurting just as much, but I had to be the responsible parent. I began taking more of an interest in Will's life, and doing what I could to be a good mom. I couldn't understand how and why Bill could check out. He was not ready to give up some of the things that masked his grief. I did what I could to share my feelings and encourage him without causing a huge argument, but I was angry because I couldn't just check out whenever I wanted. I realized that it took more time for Bill to make the choice to be present again than it took me.

It may be difficult to think of how your actions affect your relationship with your spouse and other family members, because you just need to get some sort of relief from the grief in your life. Every relationship is different, and I believe both people have to continuously work to help each other, guide each other, and remember why you became a couple.

We were grateful that some of our other family members came to be by our side, but it didn't take away the pain. We appreciated all the help with our son, Will, and all that they did for us. Yes, they also grieved the loss of Quinn, but in a different way. They loved him too, yet we lost our son who was a part of us and depended on us to help him live a safe and happy life. My relationship with our family changed, not because I loved them any less, but because I didn't think anyone could relate to my life.

Talking was too painful for a long time because the only emotion I knew was sadness. I didn't want to hear about other's accomplishments, vacations and happy stories. For a long time I thought I would never be ready to be happy again. Our family loved me and wanted me to feel joy again. I am sure it was tough for them to see me so unhappy, but it was important that they didn't push me to get back to the way things were before we lost Quinn.

This may sound strange, but I feel insulted when other parents who knew what happened to us didn't seem to learn anything from our tragedy. When I see young children riding in the front or backseat of a car without a car seat or a seatbelt, I am both angry and sad.

It feels unfair knowing my children were always belted in and other parents get away with putting their child at risk. Some parents ignore things as simple as letting their child ride a bike without a helmet or allowing a child to ride in a friend's car without enough seatbelts. This shouldn't even be an option. I think most people don't think it can happen to them and their family.

Learn from the terrible events that happen in life. Not everyone will be given a second chance.

Don't Judge the Family for Their Religious or Spiritual Thoughts

You may not agree with what a grieving parent may say or do, but remember not to judge them. They may have practiced a religion, and have decided not to go back to their church. They may have decided to try a new religion, or become interested in a new spiritual path. You are not in the same place they are, and can't wave a magic wand to take away their pain.

Our family grew up Catholic, some practicing, some not. We were angry at religious people telling us that my son and father's deaths were part of God's plan. What about our plan to raise and watch our sons grow up together until they were ready to be out on their own? Everyone has a right to believe what they want, and we wanted to believe our loved ones were in a beautiful place. Believing this didn't make the pain any less though, because, of course, the place I wanted them to be was right here with me.

I never thought much about life after death. When you lose a child all you do is think about where they are, how they are, and what they're are doing. After reading all the grief books I could find and stories of other people's losses, I explored books about the afterlife. I read books about famous mediums that included stories about people making contact from the other side. As a parent I wanted to explore anything that might give me a chance of contacting my son. I consider myself an intelligent person with an open mind and willing to learn and grow. So when I researched mediums who said they could prove they could contact loved ones who have passed, I became a true believer. Ask yourself if you would do anything to have another connection with someone you love and have lost?

Sure, there are people I will call "quacks" who may wear a bandana, look into a crystal ball and promise to deliver the information they know we want to here. I think their service should be listed for fun or entertainment purposes only. What I believe in and am talking about are real people with gifts who can communicate with spirits from the afterlife. Unless you have read the books, watched the documentaries, and attended a reading, then you should not judge a grieving parent for believing.

Our day finally came to have a reading. The session lasted about two hours. The information we received from this medium was met with mixed emotions. Some information was general, but a lot more information came with details that the medium would never have known. She was able to give us messages from our son and tell us personal information only we would know (a validation or confirmation statement). She sent messages from relatives who passed and was able to describe pets that had passed on.

I was taking notes during the reading and she asked me about the present my son made for me that I was holding. Because this was a phone reading, she had no way of seeing me, or knowing what was in my hand. The present I was holding was a pen Quinn made for me that I was using to take notes. It gave us a sense of peace that our son was being taken care of and happy on the other side.

There was one problem with getting information from the other side. The sense of peace I mentioned didn't last very long. All I wanted was more. I wanted more communication and messages from my son and dad. I craved the connection I had with them during my reading. It carried me through a few days, but then I felt I needed more. I compare getting messages to doing crack. Although I have never used the drug, I have been told after you try it, you want more and more. I needed more connections to my son, and I yearned for another reading. The idea of not having any control over communicating with my child devastated me. I can say that I did the right thing by having a reading. I treasure all the messages I received, and am very grateful to the woman who is blessed with this wonderful gift.

We did go on to have other readings. One amazing reading was given to us by a very gifted man, John Holland. At that time, Will was seeing a wonderful grief therapist named Ana. She knew of our beliefs and interest in communicating with my son and dad, and she informed us of a conference being held in Phoenix. It was a conference focused on life after death.

There were many different speakers, authors, and mediums participating in the conference. We attended a very large group where someone we had never heard about was speaking. It was a day we will be forever grateful for and never forget. Out of a few hundred people our son and my dad decided we needed to be contacted. As John Holland began to receive messages from spirit, he asked some questions, and I knew immediately he was talking about our son, Quinn. I will be forever grateful to John Holland for using his gift to bring us messages from our son who we miss so much, and I am happy to share this story.

The week before we left on our family vacation, my son and I began painting a mural on his bedroom wall. Quinn was very creative, and had so many ideas of what he wanted. We began by painting on the wall behind Quinn's door. Because Quinn never returned home with us his room is incomplete. I have never continued painting or even taken the blue tape off the baseboard where we began painting. I often look at his wall and remember how proud he was that he was a part of this mural. He painted an amazing path through the wooded area we were working on, and added some bark on the tree. Also I am not surprised at how many green plants and shrubbery he wanted. Green was his favorite color. Many different tubes of green paint still remain unused in his dresser drawer. Quinn and I talked about what other things we would add when we got back from our vacation. Unfortunately I have lost my desire to paint, and something I once loved doing is now painful.

During the time John Holland was reading for us, it was as if Quinn was guiding him through our house and upstairs to his room. My husband and I were amazed at what he told us. He said that Quinn was showing him his room, and John asked us if the painting was on the bottom of the wall. He went through the motions of reaching out to grab Quinn's door handle, and even reached out on the correct side. Next he motioned as if he was walking through

Quinn's door and immediately turned to the left and crouched down to the exact spot where we had started painting on Quinn's wall. No one else could have possible known that Quinn and I started a mural in his room. We never told anyone about it.

Quinn's mural

The following is a letter my husband and I wrote for the May 2014 edition of Parents United in Loss newsletter. We were asked to write about some of the validations we have received about our son, Quinn.

Stories of Validation-Quinn Levi

Our journey to find answers to questions that are seemingly unanswerable began on July 3, 2010 when a rollover vehicle crash took the lives of our beloved 8-year-old son, Quinn, and his grandfather, Pappy. Four more of us were in the vehicle: Quinn's Mom (Susanne), his Dad (Bill), his brother (Will), and his grandmother. We were told of Quinn and Pappy's death while recovering from our injuries in our hospital rooms. Like all of us who are members of Helping Parents Heal, we now know the all-consuming grief that the loss of a child has on the physical and mental state of the surviving parents. As a result, we lost the desire to live in a world that could take such a remarkable child. We knew that we could not give up completely, and that we had to try to find joy in life again - if not for ourselves, for our surviving son. The only thought that gave us strength was the possibility that we might see Quinn again. As impossible as this sounded, we had to know if there was a way to communicate with him. Our first experience with trying to prove that life continues after death was to read every available book that was devoted to the concept of 'Life after Death'. While these books provided hope that life continues after death, they told other people's stories and we needed proof from our own son Quinn. This led to our contact with our first medium. We found Laurie Campbell as a recommended medium on Allison Dubois' website. We were amazed by some of the things she told us. Laurie Campbell knew specifics about our son, such as his sensory disability, the horse he loved to visit in occupational therapy, his artistic ability, and even the fact that Susanne was holding something in her hand during the reading that Quinn had made for her. This was in fact a phone reading, and Susanne was writing notes with the pen Quinn had made for her. Many other things that Laurie mentioned were equally impressive. We discovered that having a good reading created an insatiable urge to have more. Much like drug users, we became addicted to hearing messages from our child. We found that we continued to want to get readings until we were finally given the one message that was definitive proof that there is truly a life after death. Our next memorable reading was with John Holland in April of 2012 in Arizona.

While attending the International Conference on After Death Communications in Scottsdale, we participated in a group session with John Holland. We were chosen out of hundreds of people to receive a message from our son and Pappy. John began receiving messages, asking audience members if the information pertained to them. After a few messages from Spirit, we knew he was speaking about our son. We raised our hands and he turned to us. The first thing he said was that they (Quinn & Pappy) were making him aware that there was an impact, meaning a car crash. He then described Quinn's personality, the specific toys he loved to play with and details of his injuries during the accident. He also knew that it had been about a year and a half since they passed, that our younger son had survived and even Susanne's father's hobby of playing cards and his service in the Navy. John also asked Bill about his shoulder and whether he had blown out his shoulder or his rotator cuff. Having suffered a rotator cuff injury during the rollover accident, Bill was astounded. Another amazing thing that John described was a phenomenon that he called 'remote viewing'. He was able to see things in his mind as if he was staring directly at them. In two such instances he referred to two different areas in our home. The first visualization was of the toys and items that we put around Quinn's urn. John was visually making a circle in the air to show where all of the toy soldiers and items were placed around Quinn's urn. The second visualization was of Quinn showing him his room. He asked about the coloring on the bottom of the wall. As John described this, he reached out in the air for the door handle, walked into Quinn's room and bent down precisely where Quinn and Susanne had begun to paint a mural the week before the accident. John relayed that Quinn said, "Look John, that's not even washed off." We knew that Quinn was with John, showing him where Susanne and Quinn had painted together.

The final medium that had a huge impact on our belief was Susanne Wilson. In addition to repeating some of the things other mediums had said, Susanne was the medium who gave us the definitive answers from Quinn that proved that he was real, and that we did not need to continue our search. During the reading, Susanne explained that she would often get a visual of a person, place or thing and that it could mean different things. For instance, she explained that if she was supposed to get a name, she might see a famous actor with the same name or initials. It was at this moment that she asked, "What is the significance of the actor Aidan Quinn?" Bill was stunned for a moment. This was the sign he had been searching for all along. He needed a medium to say Quinn's name. As much as we already believed that Quinn could communicate through mediums, Susanne Wilson gave us something Bill had asked for that was personal to him and to Quinn. We asked and he delivered, and now we will wait out the rest of our days doing the best we can for our surviving son until we see our loved ones in heaven again.

-Written by Quinn's parents and Pappy's daughter and son-in-law, Susanne and Bill Levi

Support Groups and More

Many groups were suggested, and we did try some, but finding the right fit was not easy. Any loss is devastating to a family, I needed to be around people who had experienced the loss of a child.

We attended groups where parents were grieving the miscarriage of their child. We experienced a group where the majority of the people attending had suffered the loss of an adult child, or an aging parent. We were so deep in grief over the loss of our young son, who we loved and lived with for less than nine years, that hearing from parents about a loss we couldn't relate to was not helping us. I knew they were grieving their loss and felt great sadness for them, but we needed a group who could relate to our own loss.

It wasn't until we attended the Life After Death Conference in Phoenix that we were introduced to an amazing group of people from the support group, Parents United in Loss. They approached us after witnessing our amazing reading from John Holland earlier that day.

This group is formerly known as Helping Parents Heal and is dedicated to helping parents meet others who have experienced the loss of a child, providing them with support and resources to aid with their healing process. This group allows an open discussion of parent's spiritual experiences and provides an opportunity for an open discussion of the afterlife. Everyone is welcome regardless of their religious or non-religious beliefs.

My husband and I were surprised to see what this group was all about when we attended our first meeting. I remember being welcomed as we entered the building and having a seat in one of the chairs set in a circle. As I listened to other parents speak about their children, I felt their pain and wanted them to know mine. For the next few meetings, I could not speak, all I could do was sit with a shattered look on my face and sometimes cry. As the months went on, I began to feel these people were on my team, and were there to listen and offer anything they could to help. It never gets easier to tell the story of how I lost my child, but being with other parents who have experienced the same loss made me feel like I wasn't alone.

Sharing my anger and sadness, and listening to others made me feel less alone. Sometimes just a hug from another mom or dad who was sharing the same grief was what helped me get through another day. I listened to stories of offensive and insensitive things people said to them about their visible grief over their child. Hearing about how they intended to honor their child's memory along with stories of signs they received from their child. It was comforting, and we could all relate to what it was they were saying. I knew very early on I was in the right place, but I did question the emotions of some other parents. I judged them for being able to smile, laugh and share stories without sobbing as I did. It took me a few years, but I now understand why and how they could feel that comfortable to be able to share something other than sadness.

Now when I attend this support group, I see how I was that parent who hangs their head, so engulfed in grief that they are stuck in believing life will not get any better. Life changes, and there will always be bad days, but I am in a better place now knowing where my child is, and that we will be together again someday.

Dog Therapy

From a very young age I remember having dogs in my life. For me there is something about a dog that is comforting. Dogs don't judge, yell, or kick us when we are down. At least, this has been my experience with all the dogs in my life.

I lost my first family dog when I was in 7th grade. My parents rescued Pierre when I was very little. I remember sobbing on my bed and holding onto Pierre's collar when my mom told me he was gone. To this day, I still have his collar. He was a fun, loving and sometimes sassy pet, but he was always there for me in good times and bad.

Our next family pet, Brandy came to us when I was in high school. I never thought Pierre could be replaced, and he couldn't, but Brandy earned our love and trust and was now part of our family. When I was married and moved to Arizona, it was hard leaving our family and friends. However, I had a very difficult time saying goodbye to Brandy. I was in a new state away from almost everybody I knew, and I had no canine companion to sit with me and let me know everything would work out.

Chili Pepper, my first dog adopted in Arizona, was a wonderful gift at a time when I needed some extra love in my life. He knew when I was down, and gave me a reason to smile. He was there when I brought both boys home from the hospital for the first time, and was curious about these tiny new humans. He watched over them, entertained them, and alerted me if he heard them cry. I knew from watching the boys interact with Chili that they too welcomed the love and protection Chili provided.

Quinn and Will with Chili Pepper

After the accident our two dogs were Chili and Little 'C'. They almost never left my side. When I arrived back at my sister's home from the hospital, they were waiting to greet me, but did so with gentle nudges and followed me where ever I went. Whether I was lying in bed, or sitting on the couch, the feel of my pups at my side made me feel less alone. It was if they could read my grief and wanted me to know they understood. All the times that I broke down, they were there to lick my tears. My dogs are part of my family and provide me with the best ongoing therapy available.

Journal Entry –

Chili Pepper followed me to my room like he always does. When I left your room I began to cry harder. Chili looked at me with sad eyes. I wish dogs could talk. Maybe he could say to me "you're ok." He crawls up into my arms and puts his little puppy head near mine, and across my arm. I can hear you say. "Oh what a sweet puppy. "Chili loves you Mom." I really wish you were here to say it. I miss hearing your voice. I miss seeing your blue eyes. I miss putting you to bed every night and getting you out of bed in the morning. Now that it is colder, I can remember how I used to put socks on you to warm you up. I have been doing it to Will, and I would give anything to be getting you up in the morning ready for school. I feel like a half of a person. Why would this happen? Why would we get the miracle of your life for only eight years? Why were you taken away? It's NOT FAIR!

Dogs bring an energy that says *I am here to please you, comfort and be there for you.* A creature so unselfish that a pat on the back is reward enough, but they give more than twice the love back to us. Dogs give free therapy, no payment needed. A treat or ball every now and then gives them joy and, unconditional appreciation.

So many rescues have amazing pups that are ready to be the best dog therapists around. All of our dogs have been rescue dogs, and they make great companions. I love my pups, and even though I rescued them, they continue to rescue me.

Dragonfly Reassurance

About a week before we left for Vacation I was watching the boys in our pool when a dragonfly came to visit. Quinn was fascinated by insects and flying critters, and he wanted to see if he could catch it, so he could see it up close. I warned him how difficult it may be to catch one, but he was determined to succeed. For a while the dragonfly landed on our basketball hoop rim, it hovered over our heads, and then settled down again on one of the dragonfly decorations next to the pool.

Quinn stood as still as a statue with his arms up, waiting patiently for the dragonfly to land on his hand. I couldn't believe my eyes when it happened. I ran inside to get my phone to take a picture, and when I came out it was still there. Quinn felt so proud, and my heart was so happy for him.

This dragon fly stayed for a while, and I was so glad to capture this amazing image. The memory of Quinn smiling and being so happy that he was able to get the dragonfly to land on him is something I think about every time I see one. Will, as the little brother wanted to do everything his big brother did, but unfortunately the dragonfly wouldn't land on his arm.

Quinn with his dragonfly

The next summer, swimming in our pool was difficult and sad for me. It didn't feel right and the silence at times was painful. My husband couldn't stand the quiet, so he put the radio on. This was also difficult, because whenever I heard a song that Quinn liked, it only made me miss him more. Will no longer had his brother to play games with, and there were no equal teams with just the three of us, but gradually we began to play with Will in the pool. When one of us was falling apart, the other had to step in and remember that Will was also missing his brother.

A year later it was once again summer and the three of us were out in the pool, and it was less difficult to give Will the attention he deserved. As we were hanging out in our pool, a welcome distraction flew in to visit. We all stopped to watch where the dragonfly would land first. This was Will's chance to experience what his brother had a week before he passed away.

It was amazing how long this dragonfly stayed around. First it landed on the basketball hoop rim, and then on the dragonfly decoration by our pool just as Quinn's dragonfly had done. Will carefully walked over to the edge of the pool and extended his hand toward the dragonfly. At first nothing happened, and we were all able to study every part of this beautiful insect. But soon the dragonfly took flight only to land on its next resting spot.

Just as Quinn had experienced a few years before, Will was now experiencing the same awesome accomplishment. This beautiful dragonfly flew over and landed on Will's hand. Happy tears were shed as I saw the same smile and sparkle in Wills eyes.

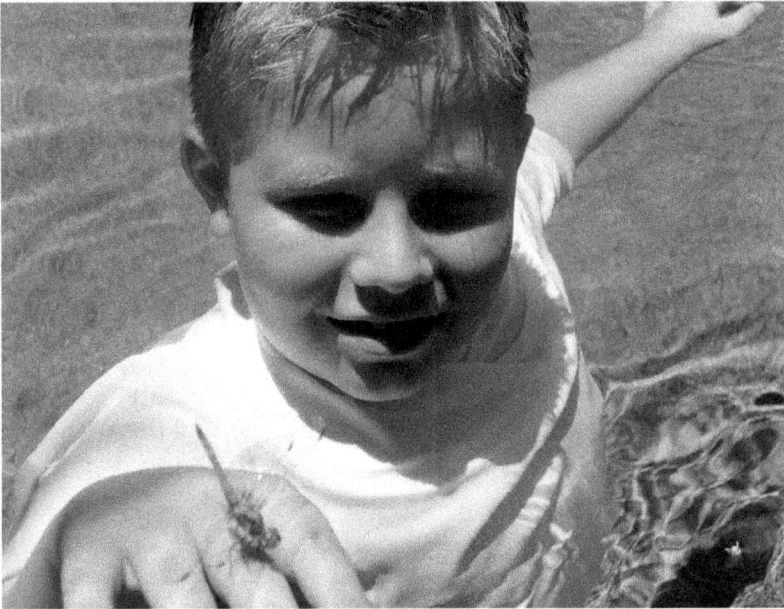

Will with his dragonfly

Was this an amazing coincidence? Maybe, but we all feel it is a sign that Quinn sent to us. From that day on, whenever we see a dragonfly not only do we feel Quinn was near, but he is always going to be with us.

My husband shared an amazing experience about what happened in the first few weeks of returning to work after the accident. Part of his job required him to travel longer distances outside of our local area, and the following happened on his first long distance trip.

At the start of the trip, before even getting on the highway, he needed to pull over into a shopping center, because he began having a panic attack. After sitting for a while, he forced himself to resume the trip to Prescott. During the ride, he had a vision of the accident flashing through his mind. As he relived the accident scene, he wondered if another highway accident was about to occur leading to his death.

As he exited the highway, he felt another panic attack coming on. Once again, he pulled over into a supermarket parking lot. He needed to gather his thoughts, so he sat there for quite some time. Opening his windows, he hoped the fresh air would help calm his nerves.

Out of nowhere, a dragonfly flew in the passenger side window. The dragonfly hovered inside of the car over the passenger side seat while Bill watched in awe. This had never happened before. Instantly, he felt calm. He believes this was Quinn's way of reassuring him that everything would be ok.

CHAPTER 9

Dos and Don'ts to Support Family and Friends

Quinn ice fishing with Cheez-It's

What to Say and Do for Parents in Grief

Journal Entry –

I have not written in this journal in a while. I have been putting my misery into a book. I don't know if it will ever be a book, but I guess it's what I wish other people would know about my life. My miserable life! It's what they should or could do, or not do. It makes me remember what my life was before this disaster happened. It's really sad, but my life as it was is over, and the new less of a person, me, is all that's left.

What happens to a parent when they have just lost their son or daughter? They live in a fog. Many days are filled with disbelief, sadness, anger, numbness, and yes, thoughts of suicide. At least this was true for my husband and me. We knew we were good parents, and we did everything to make our children's lives better, so we questioned, why us?

No one can answer that question. So my advice to you is don't try to answer it for the grieving parents and family. Don't try to tell them you understand. Honestly you don't and can't, because you haven't lost what they've lost. Don't tell them to be happy they have another child, or that they have each other. Don't tell them that God has a plan. I want to know if this God is so great how could he take away my son and father? How can taking away my eight-year-old son be part of anyone's plan?

Please don't ask a parent the question, "How are you?" Every time someone asked me how I was, I wanted to scream. Sometimes I just looked at them, sometimes I grunted, and sometimes I managed to say, "Not good." It's better to say something like, "I can't imagine how you feel," "You're in my thoughts," or "There are no words," because that parent can't be feeling good.

I think a lot of people just don't know what to say, and so they say the first thing that comes to mind, but it may sound insensitive to the parent. I believe one cannot truly understand how intensely painful it is to lose a child until they've experienced it. No one can imagine how it is to wake up each day without your child, or sit at the dinner table with an empty chair, or have your other child say, "I wish my brother didn't die, I don't like being alone."

Be there for the grieving parent even if it means to just sit in silence. Everyone grieves differently, but nothing will ever be the same for someone who has lost a child.

Many parents have a difficult time seeing other people for a long time or seeing anyone who has a connection to their child. I remember how my son used to greet our friends when they came over, how he played with their children, or what kind of picture he drew for them.

Being a good friend means being patient and not falling off the radar after a few months. It is going to take a long time for some parents to want to do some of the things they did in the past. Somethings they may never want to do again. So you can always ask, but don't be offended when they just can't.

A good friend should always check in. Make a note on your calendar to give the family a call, even if it's just to say that you thought about them that day. I can't tell you how many times my doorbell rang and when I opened the door we would find food, notes, flowers, books, or toys for Will- just something to let us know that they cared. They cared enough to respect how painful it was just to see almost anyone. So don't forget about them, but do have patience to wait until they are ready to see you again.

What can you do for the parents and family members that have lost a child? You can leave a meal at their door; ring the bell and leave. You can send them a text without needing a response. You can leave a message without expecting them to pick up the phone. You can do something for the family without asking "Let me know if there is anything I can do for you." If you feel comfortable enough to help out, then do it.

I had some wonderful friends and neighbors who came by, grabbed some cleaning supplies and went to work. Life goes on around the grieving family, but just getting out of bed is all I could manage some days. I didn't think about the dust, dirty bathrooms, or even running the dishwasher. Our friends and neighbors were very much needed and appreciated even though we couldn't express it.

I appreciated our friends who came over, gave a quick hug, got busy changing sheets, doing laundry, and running the vacuum. Then they'd say, " I'll be back again," as they walked out the door. I felt uncomfortable and couldn't hold in my emotions whenever I saw someone, so I appreciated that they respected me enough to do what they could without expecting anything in return-yes, not even a thank you.

I used every bit of energy I had to do what I could for Will. Will was only five at the time he lost his brother and grandfather. When you are five years old and your parents are sitting around crying, and you don't have your brother to play with, you are confused and angry. So another helpful thing to do is offer to watch children, or take them outside to play. Many times good friends came by to take Will out of the house for a few hours. It was good for my husband and I to know he was taken care of and away from our constant sadness. You can drop off activities the child can do by himself when his parents are falling apart. Most importantly, without forgetting about them, you can give parents all the time they need to attempt to live again when they are ready.

Here are two lists to recap what I've said about how to help parents in grief.

DON'T and DO List

DON'T	DO
*Ignore the family	*Text, call or leave a message
*Tell them you understand	*Tell them you can't imagine how they feel
*Say it is God's plan	*Be there to listen
*Say this will get better, or this will pass	*Be patient
*Avoid the family	*Say or use the child's name
*Be pushy	*Offer to help with the children
*Think it's wrong to use the child's name	*Drop off food or snacks
*Think they will want to cook, or have food.	*Help with tasks such as get their mail, walk their dogs, or mow their lawn
*Assume they are thinking about simple tasks	*If they are accepting visitors, be present with the grieving parents, being a body in the room is enough
*Be uncomfortable with silence.	*Support and accept that the parents will never be "back to normal."
*Think that they will "get over it."	*Check in
*Forget	

Friends Share Their Grief Journey

When people came to see me after my son and father died, I didn't think there was anything anyone could say or do for me. For a long time I avoided seeing people because it was too hard not to feel the sadness they felt for me. It was overwhelming and intensely painful for me to face family, friends and neighbors. I was no longer the fun, friendly mom I was before I lost my son.

I have been introduced to many parents over the past few years who also grieve over the loss of their child. I asked if they were willing to share a story, sentence, word, comment good, bad or both that people have said to them throughout their grief journey. I met some amazing people because of the tragedy that happened in our lives. I wish I never knew them, but I am still thankful I do. Here are some of the responses I received.

I met this wonderful woman because of my son. Here is what she shared.

I guess what has affected me the most that comes to mind is not so much what people have said to me but rather the guilt I feel when posed the question, "Do you have any siblings,?" and my response is always, "I am the youngest of three, I have an older sister and my older brother was killed when I was very young." Then they always say, "I am so sorry," and they feel bad for asking, but I don't want them to feel bad for asking... I just wish they felt like they didn't have to feel bad for asking me! It is very important for me to not ignore that yes, I do have a brother... he's just not here anymore. So that has been a constant struggle over the years... just to put people at ease for asking and allowing me to freely talk about my brother without making them feel bad!

The following is written by a friend from our Parents United in Loss group:

For me, it's not so much the words that I was hurt by from others, it was what they did. Before we lost the twins we had six miscarriages. I remember going back to work and many of the people I had worked with for years acted "normal" and said nothing. I'm sure it was awkward for them, not knowing what to say, and they "didn't want to upset me" but it came across to me as if they interpreted my loss as nothing worth mentioning. Just one sentence would have validated that they knew and cared about my loss. I felt even more alone with our grief.

After losing my daughter, I could feel someone cared and acknowledged how devastated we were (are) with a look, an "I'm so sorry" (even though cliché, it expressed that they cared), and especially with a hug. And for those more in our inner circle, showing up was the most meaningful way others could reach out to us. Arriving home after being at the hospital, neighbors arrived at the door with hugs. My dad and brother came over immediately. A dear friend stepped up and became our extra brain, personal assistant, and guide as we had to maneuver our way through the arrangements and afterwards. Another friend set up a fundraiser to help cover expenses. Another friend set up meal deliveries. Another friend helped me with the program for the celebration of life, and my brother helped me record music for it. Two friends sang and played guitar. One of my brother-in-laws flew in for us.

The disappointments were in people who didn't show up, one way or another. One relative who I would have thought was the most sensitive one, who, six months later, when he was in town, told me he never called because he just didn't know what to say. "Really?" Another friend didn't come to the service, because he didn't see the information about it on Face- book. Another close friend went on a trip with her boyfriend, saying his grandmother was dying. She wasn't. Anyway, I truly appreciated those who stepped up.

As far as grieving "too long" most of my crying has been when I'm alone or when I would drive my surviving daughter to school. I don't think anyone told me I should be done grieving by any certain time. My sister-in-law did encourage me to "get something (like a hobby) just for me," and one of my friends would ask me if I had done anything to enrich myself lately. Both were not trying to push me, just to encourage me to allow myself to find some joy.

Ultimately, what did help me was to take time to appreciate Spring, take pictures of beauty, then to start painting. So, beauty saved me. Or at least helped pull me out of the darkness. I am generally pretty private about losing my daughter, on Facebook and in real life, but I do feel good about honoring her. With Parents United in Loss I am reminded we are not the only "good people who don't deserve this type of devastation," but the sadness of the other losses is tough to hear about. The concept that our children are still alive in spirit is the bright spot that helped me to leave another grief group, and to think beyond the grief. It is so subtle and intangible that it's hard for me to feel 100% sure 100% of the time. But then how would mediums know what they know?

This next mom told me that no one has ever said a negative thing to her regarding her grief process. She was thankful for this, because she said her response would not be controlled.

She feels that ever since she decided to make her sons Birthdays and Angeliversaries a BIG deal by doing "pay it forward in honor of him," it has brightened up people's lives. This mom says that it grounds them and doing something kind for someone else makes them realize life is too short. Both grieving friends and non-grieving friends pay if forward on her sons birthdays and angel dates. So basically she is choosing to celebrate her son and by including everyone and anyone that she knows it makes her son HAPPY AND PROUD of his mom.

Be Observant

When a parent feels so low and is at the point of not wanting to get off the couch, friends and family may stop by to visit. They want to cheer up the person grieving, and that's understandable. Please remember that when someone is grieving, they probably don't want to make small talk. They don't want to hear about the local attractions they visited, how much they enjoyed themselves, and the gifts they purchased to take home with them for their family members. They have just lost someone close to them, and can't imagine enjoying themselves again.

Sometimes just being a body in the room is enough. I think people feel that they have to say something so there isn't silence in the room. Don't worry about uncomfortable silence. Sometimes you can help best by passing the tissue box, or offering to make them food, or give them a glass of water. Just go get them a snack, and put it in front of them. They will eat if they want it.

Be careful not to become too comfortable and lose yourself, or laugh hysterically at the TV. When this happened to me, I thought, *How insensitive can they be when I am suffering and they are laughing away?* There is a time for laughter, but laughter isn't always the best medicine. Pay attention to what will be appropriate. This is true, especially early in grieving. I know we didn't watch much television, and especially not the news. Hearing news about other accidents, deaths, and senseless crimes only depressed me more. Be observant of body language, and remember this is a tender time for those grieving.

Because we were limited by our injuries we spent a lot of time on the couch. Sometimes the T.V. was on to break the silence in the room, but mostly Will played video games to keep himself busy while we sat and watched, trying our best to be present to him. For the first time Will, like many children had never witnessed his parents grieve in this way. It is completely normal to cry and show emotion in front of children. With parents grieving the loss of a child, the challenge comes when it may be necessary to do your best and take some time to be with your surviving child. As much as we wanted to stay in bed and sleep all day until this nightmare was over, we had to be present for our son. All you can do is try.

I think we tried because we realized that Will was experiencing this with us. He lived through this accident, and he lost who we lost. It was a confusing time for him, and being so young, his emotions were all over the place. He processed it differently, but still needed to be a kid, and do the things kids do.

We appreciated the people that came by to take Will out of the house so he could be with other kids. Will was never an only child, and not having Quinn in the house was difficult. He never asked for any of this, and so as much as we were numb, we were observant and did what we could for Will.

CHAPTER 10

Quinn's Treasures

Will looking at Quinn's memorial brick at Sierra Verde School

What is Sensory Processing Disorder?

Sensory processing disorder (SPD) is a condition in which the brain has trouble receiving and responding to information that comes through our senses. Some people are over-sensitive and so sounds that they hear every day can be painfully loud and overwhelming. Multiple senses may be affected by SPD, like hearing, touch or taste. Sensory processing problems can affect adults, but are usually identified in children. Children with sensory processing disorder are some of the most misdiagnosed, misguided and misunderstood children. If recognized in young children, it can be treated before they are blamed and judged. If not, learning becomes too difficult, for the child, and they are likely to isolate and annihilate themselves.

Imagine feeling like your shirt or socks are three times too small, or your shoes are squeezing your feet so tight they are cutting off circulation. A child with SPD might feel this way. To the average child, if someone walked by them and bumped into them, they might get startled but would be able to shake it off. When Quinn was bumped, it felt like a hammer hit him. All or some of the senses are on overload when you have SPD.

We all have used a public restroom where the toilets have sensors and flush automatically, right? The flush can be loud and might even startle you. Imagine hearing that flushing sound three times as loud. Until Quinn was diagnosed, starting the lawn mower without warning would send him running to hide under the table. These are just some examples of Quinn's sensory issues.

Have you ever been in a quiet room but couldn't focus because you heard the buzzing of fluorescent lights or the ticking of a clock? Try turning up the volume a lot, and you may have an idea of how difficult it can be for someone with SPD to concentrate. Every-day routines such as sleeping, brushing your teeth, wearing clothes, riding on a noisy bus, sitting still in a chair or standing for a long time are often not routine for children with SPD.

Think about how you would feel if your clothes felt like they were made of sand paper, certain smells made you nauseous, lights feel so bright that they cause a headache, whispers sound like yells, and writing is difficult because too much pressure is applied or it takes too long to make your hand form the letter correctly. Some of these things may sound easily manageable, but for someone with SPD they are not.

As Quinn's parents, we did everything we could to help Quinn overcome his sensory issues. We notified all of his teachers and gave suggestions on ways to make his school day more manageable, and had him in occupational therapy, which helped in many areas.

The biggest improvement came from what we discovered after talking to a friend at our neighborhood park in May of 2010. We discovered a brain training program that offered hope at tackling Quinn's sensory issues. We saw enough proof after observing her son run, play, and do things that should have been very limiting for him to accomplish.

We went home that night and checked the web site for The Cognitive Center for Enhancement. I made the call the next day and got Quinn signed up to start the program. Quinn started this program right after his second grade school year ended. He wouldn't live to finish the program, or to show his classmates and teachers the amazing changes he was working so hard to accomplish. We were so hopeful that this was going to give Quinn the ability to get his sensory issues under control and make everyday things easier for him to participate in. With the amazing changes we saw after only a month in the program we know it was working.

Some of the areas we hoped the training would help Quinn were: improved attention, cognitive processing, increasing his mental strength, improved adaptability and to have more self-confidence. Quinn worked hard at the program even though in the beginning it was a struggle and way outside of his comfort level. With each appointment he knew what to expect and became less uncomfortable gearing up for his session.

The last week of Quinn's life we observed him enjoy being more free of the sensory issues that had been weighing down who he was to become. The good and sometimes bad smells of the ocean and beach didn't send him into sensory overload. Applying sunscreen didn't make his skin feel like it was being attacked. Sitting on the beach with the sand sticking to him didn't stop him from enjoying the day. We were convinced that the program was working. We were overjoyed that Quinn had some relief from the sensory issues that were limiting him.

The Center for Cognitive Enhancement uses research and applied technology together to enhance health and performance of the brain. For more information on brain training go to The Center for Cognitive Enhancement.

Alexa Honors Quinn

When Quinn was in first grade I'd often see him giving a hug to a tall eighth grade, blond girl as he walked out of the gate from school. One day I asked him, "Who is that pretty girl you are always giving hugs to?" He said, "Oh mom, that's my friend, Alexa." I learned some more about Alexa from Quinn's teacher, Debbie. Alexa babysat for Debbie's son, and she knew her well. Quinn always smiled when he saw her.

We were always looking for ways to help Quinn with his sensory issues. He was so smart, but we wanted to strengthen the skills that gave him difficulty. After talking with Quinn's teacher, we decided that Alexa would be a great resource to help Quinn. Quinn loved his teacher, she understood him, and he trusted her. He was very comfortable with Alexa, and was more than excited when he found out she would come to our house to work with him.

Of course Quinn wanted to treat it as more of a play date than a tutoring session. I remember him taking her up to his room to show her around. He told me to go downstairs and get some refreshments. Quinn was always the best host, offering guests drinks and snacks. When I came upstairs, he took the snacks and ushered me out of the room. He wanted all of Alexa's attention.

She worked on reading and writing activities, and I know Quinn probably did his best to avoid the work so they could just socialize. Alexa had to be patient with Quinn, as sometimes his sensory issues sent him into a meltdown. I knew Quinn enjoyed her time, so much that he would want her to stay and hangout with him for the rest of the day like they were best buds. Even though Alexa was almost ten years older, he wasn't shy.

I wouldn't know the true impact Quinn left on Alexa until after he passed away. I was notified by email about something she did to honor him. Alexa was awarded a basketball scholarship to the University Of Hawaii. I received a picture of her basketball shoes. On the tongues of her shoes she had printed, "PLAY 4 QUINN."

Alexa's basketball shoes

This instantly brought happy tears to my eyes. For someone as young as Alexa to honor my son in this amazing way, meant more than anyone could know. She was away from her family and friends, starting college, and with all she had to think about and do, she remembered Quinn. I wished I could fly to Hawaii, hug her for Quinn, and see all of her games. One thing I know for sure is that Quinn is proud of her, and watching and cheering her on each and every time she plays.

Treasured Writings from Quinn

*You are as sweet as a heart. Happy Mother's Day

*When I'm in high school, I would like to be the richest person ever. When I'm 25, I hope I will own a lego factory.

*My family is special because I love them.

*I work very hard to make my mom happy.

*My parents are the best because they play, read and go places. We play army guys; we read in bed, we go to the beach. I like to play, read and go places with my mom and dad.

*Dear Tooth Fairy,

Can I please keep my tooth? I want to have it forever. And would you please give some money to me.

I. ♡ U. Thank you-Quinn

*I love you because you share chocolate ice cream.

*My mom can do many things! I think she's best at being super nice and excellent.

*My mom is the best mom on the planet.

*She is the best mom at cooking.

* I'd like to tell my mom that I love her.

Finishing this book

I truly wish I didn't ever have a reason to write this book. Maybe I thought it was good to journal and get my anger and sadness out. Maybe I thought it would help people to better understand what life is like for parents who have lost a child. Almost everyone asked us the question, what can we do? I didn't think anyone could do anything for us, but there are plenty of things that you can do, you just can't make the pain go away.

Treasure your family every day. I am living proof that your life can be shattered in the blink of an eye without any warning. Take time for yourself, but do your job as a parent. What is more important than your family? If you took on the responsibility of becoming a parent then do it, and love doing it.

I love being a mom. I know how my son and dad felt about me, and I can be proud. Understand why everyday things can be so difficult for the grieving family to do. If the story of my tragedy can make you rethink how you live your life then you're doing a good thing for you, your friends and your family.

I lived my life thinking of what was best for my children. I miss my son Quinn everywhere I go, and with everything I do. Now all I have left to treasure are the memories of my son that are forever frozen it time until I can see my sweet boy again in heaven. For a while after I lost my son I didn't care if I lived. My surviving son is the reason I am here. Will gives my husband and I reason to live every day. No one could take better care of him then us, and it is what we must do until we are no longer needed.

Our days are long and often filled with sad moments when we are missing Quinn. I believe it will be this way for the rest of our lives. To all the friends and family of grieving parents, I say understand that this is their new life. It isn't anything they wanted to happen or asked for. Please accept them for who they are, and know that they are doing the best they can. They will always miss and treasure the memories of their loved ones who have passed, and they will appreciate you for accepting them as they are now.

About the author

Susanne Levi, advocate for child safety, is a mom, former art teacher and volunteer for HALO (Helping Animals Live On) Animal Rescue. She taught art in the Scottsdale and Deer Valley School Districts. Susanne moved from Pennsylvania to Arizona with her husband, Bill, in 1998. They have two children, Quinn and Will.

Susanne's parents, John and Eileen Taylor, also made the move to Arizona in 2001. Shortly after that, her sister, Donna, husband, Joe, and son, Nathan, joined them. They all shared holidays, vacations and weekends together as a close-knit family. Susanne started her career teaching art in the Scottsdale school district, then moved over to the Deer Valley School District.

In 2010, while driving back from a vacation in their Trailblazer, a tragic accident took the life of Susanne's son, Quinn, and her father, John. Susanne shares her story in hopes of honoring their memory and to prevent a similar tragedy for other families.

Her book offers a better understanding of what families feel after the loss of a child, and guides friends, co-workers, neighbors and other family members in ways to comfort a grieving family.